THE FUTURE
IS
kNOWing
NETWORK
MARKETING

BY

PATRICK W. HIGGINS

"The relentless pursuit of excellence in training"

THE FUTURE IS kNOWing NETWORK MARKETING

Copyright © 1996 Patrick W. Higgins

Library of Congress
Cataloging in Publication Data
ISBN 0-9658978-1-8

Published by

Unlimited Horizons Training
111 S. Olive St., Suite #444
Media, PA 19063

(800) 300-1177

Manufactured in the United States of America

CONTENTS

PART THREE: CARING IS SHARING

PART FOUR: BUILDING FOR THE FUTURE

EPILOGUE: What is Unlimited Horizons?

PREFACE

Why I Chose Network Marketing and
Wrote This Book

Back in 1989, I was one of the most miserable people in America. My nerves were completely shot! My business was failing and I was scared to death. Things were so bad that I couldn't even sleep at night. What scared me most wasn't my immediate bills (although they frightened me!), it was foreseeing no end in sight. This terrified me! I really thought I was doomed to poverty.

The main reason my previous business was failing, was mostly due to the fact that I didn't enjoy what I was doing. I no longer had the heart for it. Honestly speaking, it was a major challenge for me just to wake up in the morning.

There was, however, one bit of hope I clung to with all my heart and soul. I knew I lived in a country where anyone could become successful if they truly wanted to. The proof? Why, it was all around me. The many mansions in the nicer sections of town. The classy automobiles driving on the roads and highways. The yachts in the marinas. The jet airplanes in the airports all over this nation, and so on.

On one particular occasion, I was at the airport in Philadelphia. I used to drive there to watch the airplanes land. This used to help relax my nerves. One day, I saw something that had an incredible impact on my life. I saw this man pull up in his new Mercedes Benz 560 SEL. As he arrived, two men opened the door to his car. One of the men removed his briefcase and garment bag, while the other man parked his car. This man had his own private jet airplane!

I stared in awe as he walked towards the aircraft. I counted as he walked up seven steps to board his plane. He then vanished into the fuselage. I stood there amazed as I watched his airplane taxi down the runway in preparation for take off. My heart was pounding! As the airplane flew out of sight, I was breathless! It was quite a spectacle! That, in my eyes, was true success.

Later that day, while on my way home, all I kept saying to myself was, "Wow! Wouldn't that be great? That's the way to really live life to its fullest. He's probably going to a first class resort somewhere in the Caribbean, and here I am driving home to a place I don't even like." When I arrived home, I took one look at the place where I was living and was immediately depressed. I thought to myself, "I gave 25 years of my life to be where I am today, and look what I've accomplished - nothing!"

This man's success had reminded me of my failure. Think about it, I was living in a lower class neighborhood, renting the first floor of a duplex. The rent wasn't paid; my bills weren't paid; I wasn't eating right; and I honestly saw no relief in sight! A feeling of disgust came over me. "I'm tired of living this way!" I said to myself. "I'm tired of this neighborhood and this city!" The sad thing was, I couldn't even afford to live this undesired lifestyle anyway!

It was obvious to me at that moment that I had a serious decision to make. I could go on living my life the way I had been living it, and continue to be broke and miserable; or I could change my life. It didn't take long for me to make up my mind. After I made the obvious choice, I immediately felt stronger. I had so much energy inside me! Imagine that! All this energy from a single decision.

The decision I made to change my life was simple; but now came the biggest problem. I knew my business could never bring me the lifestyle I had witnessed earlier at the airport. Further, I didn't know of any industry that could. I mean, what industry could take an average person like

6

myself, and give me a track to run on which would lead me to financial independence? I really didn't think one existed; but I made a commitment to myself that night to find out if one did. And if such an industry did exist, I swore I would grab it with all my might and never let it go.

Lo and behold, Network Marketing was introduced to me. Again, I would never have found this great industry had I decided to settle for the lifestyle I was living up to that point. I'm so glad I decided to make a change in my life. It was the best thing I ever did. It saved me from a life of misery and poverty.

During the opportunity presentation, I knew within the first twenty minutes that I was going to do this for the rest of my life. I just knew this was my chance to achieve the lifestyle I so desperately wanted and so richly deserved.

After I got involved, I learned there were people who owned their own jet airplanes because of this great industry. After hearing that, I immediately wondered if the man I saw at the airport that day was involved also. I never did find out. But I didn't need to! All I knew was that I finally found the industry that could bring me true success. That excited me!

Network Marketing will show you *how* to become successful too! But you have to know WHY you want to become successful. My WHY was simple - I was broke and miserable. I wanted everything life had to offer; but I didn't know how to get it. When I finally did find out *how*, I totally committed myself to this industry and immediately got busy building my future.

This industry really delivers! I can state with total confidence that it has totally changed my life. It can change your life too! Once again, after you know **where** you want to go and **why**, Network

Marketing will show you **how**. It's a miracle waiting to happen in your life, if you just let it.

The purpose for this book is to help as many people as I can become successful in Network Marketing. I'm committed to getting the truth out about this great industry! Further, I wrote this book in hopes of reaching the average person to let you know - there is hope. If I can do this business, you can too! We were all taught and trained to be average. I'm here to tell you that it doesn't have to be that way. Here is your chance to prosper.

There is no other opportunity like this in the world! I can honestly tell you that if I hadn't found Network Marketing, I probably would have been stuck in Philadelphia my whole life. This business has totally lifted my spirits, widened my horizons and helped me realize I had abilities I never dreamed I possessed.

With everything that's happened to me in the past few years, I feel obligated to this industry to produce the very best training materials I can. I didn't write this book to win any literary awards. On the contrary, it was sincerely and honestly written with you in mind. And believe me, that's more important to me than any literary awards. Awards are nice, but if the book doesn't serve its purpose, then it shouldn't have been written. It is my sincere wish for you to benefit from using it. If I help you, I am helping the industry. And that's the least I can do for what this industry has done for me.

Making money is really not that difficult once the proper foundation is laid. It's at the foundation, however, where most people fall short. The principles you're going to learn throughout this book will not only help you build a successful foundation for your Network Marketing business; if used properly, they'll also help you build a successful foundation for life. I sincerely hope you enjoy them.

INTRODUCTION

Personal Letter from the Author

On behalf of your future, I would personally like to thank you for putting your confidence in us for your Network Marketing training. I would also like to congratulate you for making the right choice. You chose the right industry - Network Marketing; and the best investment - Yourself!

Most people today would rather spend their time and money playing the lottery hoping to win financial freedom. They fail to realize, financial freedom can't be won (only a few ever do win). YOU MUST EARN IT! Even with such low odds of winning, people flock to stores nationwide in hopes of becoming overnight millionaires. However, for the most part, it's only an illusion. Let's make it clear right now! The lottery is not a good investment! But YOU are. Why? Because you can't control the lottery, but you can control yourself.

Face the facts, the 90's is the YOU decade! Therefore, you need to realize YOU are the only real investment you've got. However, purchasing this book doesn't guarantee success, but it's a great first step. Learn and duplicate this training as best you can. Put these principles to work for you right now. You'll be amazed at the results, as principles are applied.

Remember, the door of opportunity is marked PUSH. Therefore, you need to push yourself to get to the top. One way to win is to act as if it were impossible to fail. Of course, if that's too much to ask of yourself, you can always take the easy way out and go back to what you had before. Make the right choice! You're worth it, aren't you? Thanks once again. I hope this book is the big reason for your financial success.

Sincerely,

Patrick W. Higgins
Founder and C.E.O.

ACKNOWLEDGMENTS

Over the years I can honestly say that I have been greatly blessed with the people God has sent my way. There are so many people who have helped inspire me to write this book. I am so thankful for all of you. It would be impossible for me to mention everyone, so I'll only mention a few. However, for the rest of you who helped inspire me in any way, I extend my heartfelt thanks.

First, I would like to thank my Mom and Dad. If it weren't for them, I wouldn't be where I am or who I am today. This book is dedicated to them. Second, I would like to thank my son, Joseph. He is a true inspiration. He gives me so much love and makes my life complete.

Third, I would like to thank my twin brother Mike. Mike supported me when I really needed it. He never questioned me, he just did whatever he could to help. I'm so grateful. Fourth, I would like to thank my other brother Jim. He came through when I needed him most.

Next, I would like to thank some of my wonderful family and friends: George Hanitz, Brian Higgins (my brother), Bill Flores, Steve Mitchell, Dave Scott, Stuart Shanefield, Beth Gottlieb, Tom Kronberger, Kevin Higgins (my brother), Chrissy Higgins (my sister), Richard Owen, Michele Lilly, Charles Culmer, Paul Caron, Lynn Stankavich, Matthew Conley, Kathleen (Kat) Roberts, Jeffrey Bouton, Elva Parsons, Arlene O'Keefe and Jack O'Keefe, Undoubtedly, they are some of the greatest people on the planet. If there were more people like them in this world, it surely would be a better place to live. I am both honored and grateful to be (or have been) associated with them.

Next, I would like to thank my partner, best friend, and better half, Nicolett. She is the most incredible person I have ever met! I could not have written this book without her help. I truly mean that. I have never met anyone who gives as much love, support and understanding as she does. Everything she gives, she gives unconditionally. That's a rare thing these days. I look forward to a great future with her. She is one in a million.

Last but definitely not least, I would like to thank Almighty God. All praise, honor and glory goes to Him. I am so thankful for the gift He has given me. I definitely could not have written this book without Him. He runs this training company, not me. I pray that He will continue to shine on our company. I'm quite sure He will.

Part One

Network Marketing:

To Know it

is

To Love it

The only good

is knowledge

and

the only evil

is ignorance.

(Socrates)

1

Times have Changed - Have You?

Did it ever occur to you that there may be a reason why so many people fail in life? It's a fact - the vast majority (approximately 95% of us) wind up failures. Is it that some of us are born to become successful, while the majority of us are born to fail?

Why are millions of Americans crawling through life on their hands and knees while allowing the cancer of failure to spread throughout their lives? Why do all but a few of us find ourselves at age 65, dependents? Why must children provide for aged parents, when it ought to be the other way around? Why doesn't social security or retirement pensions provide these elders with enough to live on?

Did you know that at the age of 65, out of 100 people: 1 will be very wealthy; 4 will be financially secure; 10 will still be working; 49 will be broke, dependent on their families, friends and government for assistance; and the other 36 will be dead? If you were to turn 65 tomorrow, which category would you fall into?

Are you on track to retire financially independent? Or, are you like most of us who are wrestling with the problems of making ends meet? The ones who do make it big; is it chance? Destiny? Luck? Or, are there definite success principles they continually use? If there are certain success principles, what are they? Let's take a look and see.

Is College the Answer?

For some people it is. But for the majority, is it really the ticket to financial independence? If you think it is - honestly answer the upcoming question.

If college is the ticket to financial independence (like most people say it is), why is this country full of highly educated individuals who are either broke and unemployed, or working in dead end positions, hoping for the promotions they know deep down in their hearts they'll never get?

Did these people know prior to going to college that the end result for most of them would be going from business to business with a degree and a resume, practically begging to be employed by anyone who would take them in? Why is this the case? Because in college, we're not taught what we really need to learn for success. We're taught things that have absolutely no direct correlation to success.

When I do my trainings, I frequently ask the people in the audience to raise their hands if they went to college. Usually about 70% of the group will raise their hands. I then ask how many of them are actually doing what they went to college for. Usually only 5% of them keep their hands raised. Talk about sad! Further, all of these graduates agree that only a small percentage of what they were taught was ever needed in the real world. Most agreed their college years were wasted acquiring useless information.

These people (the ones who weren't doing what they paid to learn to do in college), were usually disillusioned. Think about it, they went to school for 4 years and paid a lot of money for their education, only to end up with a degree and a student loan to pay. Wouldn't you be disillusioned?

If you really think college is the answer, ask yourself this: How many people who are going to college today are actually going to make it big in the real world after they graduate? I'm sure you'll agree the number is quite slim. Twenty years ago, however, chances were much better than they are today.

Today, we're faced with 2 scary facts: First, companies are laying off thousands upon thousands of middle-management employees each month in America. This is due to company down-sizing, mergers, buy-outs, decreasing budgets, computers, etc. Second, today's educated American will switch companies 9 times in a 40-year career. Why? Because they don't want to keep us around anymore. They can't afford to!

Companies are losing millions! Still, the C.E.O.'s of these companies are giving themselves healthy annual raises. They don't care about us like they used to. The ones at the top are taking care of themselves, so if the company does go under, they'll have enough to retire on. Let's face it, unless you're at the top, you have little or no control over the company's future, or your own future for that matter.

Is Owning Your Own Business or Franchise the Answer to Success?

According to Dun and Bradstreet, 95% of the smaller independent business owners are heading towards bankruptcy. 80% of them will fail within the first year alone! Most small business owners today are scared to death! I know this personally, because I had three small businesses prior to getting involved with Network Marketing.

One of the worst feelings in the world is owning a business that you know is going to fail. The reasons for failure are many: Lack of capital, too much competition, bad location, etc. The list could go on forever. The same goes for franchising also.

A franchise, in my opinion, is just buying yourself a job. You're buying someone else's idea and paying anywhere from $100,000 to $1,000,000 for the use of it. On top of that, you need to be there 60 - 80 hours a week, because most of your employees are high school students who have little or no clue as to how to run a business. Sure you can make a lot of money, but how and when can you enjoy it?

Most people think a franchise is a guaranteed ticket to success. Not true. Look around at all of the big name franchises that are closing down. Take a walk into your local mall. How are things going there? It doesn't matter where you live in America. Fact is, retail franchise stores are hurting real bad. Not all of them, but a lot of them.

I have friends who own their own franchises. Some of them are doing well and some aren't. All of them, however, regret the fact they ever bought a franchise in the first place! Regardless of their financial status, whether it's good or bad, they all look stressed out. It looks as if they've aged 20 years in just 2 or 3 years. That's not success to me.

With a business or franchise, there are always so many crucial decisions to make. For instance, whenever you buy a business or franchise, the location is of utmost importance to you. It will make or break you! Unfortunately, even good locations suffer under certain conditions.

For instance, I know a man who owns a business in a prime retail location. He had a slow start like most people do, but eventually he built a prosperous business for himself. One day, the city decided to do repair work on the street where his business was located. He knew this would hurt his business, but there was nothing he could do to stop them.

His street was under construction for 6 months! Talk about ridiculous! For 6 months, his customers couldn't drive to his place of business for service. He was a nervous wreck. He lost a fortune and almost had to close down. He finally re-opened again when the road was finished, but the delay cost him a few of his customers. Some of the people who used to come to him found someone else instead. This poor man did nothing wrong to deserve this fate, but, once again, there was nothing he could do about it. Talk about a victim of circumstance!

Now, I'm not knocking being in business for yourself. In my opinion, working for yourself is the only way to go. This is America! The land of opportunity! The only question is, which opportunity is the right one in today's rapidly changing times? Before we answer this question, let's go back in time.

Back in Time

Twenty years ago, a college education usually meant a good career. So did owning your own business or franchise. Today, however, let's be honest - what are your chances? Not so good. For instance, if you had $200,000 to invest right now into a business, and you bought a franchise, would you feel you just purchased a guaranteed thing? Probably not. But if you did that 20 years ago, you'd be very wealthy today.

Things were so much easier back then. Even if you didn't go to college or own a business or franchise, you could still live a good lifestyle. There were plenty of good jobs out there for hard working people. Usually only one income was needed to pay the bills. The man of the house usually worked 5 days a week and had the weekends off to spend with his family.

Back then, even the military was a good career to choose. It offered an excellent benefit plan and a good retirement plan as well. So did working for the city, the state and the U.S. Government.

Back to the 90's

Today, things are much different than they used to be. The people who chose those careers back then, for the most part, are struggling today. It's not their faults. They didn't foresee this happening in the future. If they had, I'm sure most of them would have chosen different careers.

Today, the cost of living has sky-rocketed, yet salaries have increased only slightly. The people who are retired today and receiving a pension are usually working another job. Why? The answer is simple. If they couldn't pay their bills before they retired, how are they going to pay their bills on a pension, which is usually 60% of what they previously earned? The answer is - *they can't.*

That's why they're being forced out of retirement and back into the workplace. It breaks my heart to see this. It's not fair. It is, however, reality. And there is little we can do about it.

To survive today, we need at least 2 incomes coming in. Jobs, however, are very scarce. Besides, you'll never become wealthy working for someone else anyway. The people who work for others, usually work hard their whole lives, only to die broke. Face it, when you get a job, all you're doing is trading hours for a wage. You'll never become wealthy this way. Your time and your income is, and always will be, controlled.

What really happens when we work for someone is - The owners use us to help build their dreams, and then they throw us away after 30 - 40 years of hard work and pay us a few hundred dollars a month for all our efforts! That is if they don't lay us off first, or fire us. Again, it's unfair, but there's not much we can do about it. Did you know things got so bad that even the military had to lay people off? That's absurd!

I recently interviewed a man who was the Marketing Director for a non-profit organization based in Penndel, Pennsylvania, His organization raises money for deprived children throughout the Delaware Valley.

This man told me in our interview that it was next to impossible to find volunteers to help them in their cause. "People just do not have time anymore to help non-profit organizations," he said, "no matter how good the cause may be." He then added, "If you want people to help you today, you have to pay them for their time. People still love to help a good cause, but they can't afford to. The only possible way for them to contribute is if they're paid for their time."

After thinking about what he said, it made sense. Twenty years ago, people did have time to help non-profit organizations, because they didn't have to work 2 or 3 jobs just to survive!

Once again, it's very sad that things have to be this way. But there's not much we can do about it.

Times have Changed

I sure hope you can now begin to understand why the industries and jobs that helped so many people prosper in the past are no longer working today. Everything is changing! Change is inevitable. Think about it, your age changes every second, temperatures always change, relationships change, jobs change, and yes, industries change too!

The ones who accept this fact and change with the times will prosper. On the other hand, the ones who insist, "It worked this way 20 years ago, and it's going to work this way now," are not seeing things properly. These people are the ones who cling to Status Quo. Status Quo is the tendency to cling to existing conditions and avoid change.

We all grow comfortable with existing conditions. When the word change is mentioned, it scares most of us to death! We feel this way because of a fear of the unknown. People would rather stick to their current conditions in life (even if they don't like them), just to avoid change. That's why the people who are unhappy with their jobs don't quit. It's because of this fear of the unknown. They would rather be broke and miserable, than change.

The same goes for their relationships, financial situations, family arrangements, etc. Face it, times are changing whether you want them to or not! To help overcome this fear, you need to accept change. Your life is going to change whether you want it to or not. The only unknowns are **how** and **when**. You can either accept this and direct the changes, or you can have them direct you. It's up to you.

Okay, now that we know what doesn't work anymore, what does work? Is there a way out of this mess? Is there a secret to success? If I wasn't born successful, am I doomed to fail? These are all good questions. In answering them, I'm both thankful and happy to say that yes, there is a way out of this mess. And yes, there is an industry that can help you prosper in life! This industry is Network Marketing. But before we discuss Network Marketing, let's define success.

What is the Secret to Success?

There are millions of people searching for the big secret to success. Do you know why they never found one yet and why they never will? You got it! Because such a secret doesn't exist! The same simple success principles that worked 2,000 years ago still work today. However, with everything so fast paced today, people don't believe this to be true.

We all have the tendency to wave aside the obvious. The obvious, however, is where success can be found. Did you ever look for something that was right underneath you nose, and you still couldn't find it? You looked everywhere, except for the obvious place, and that's where it was. Well, the same holds true for success.

Success is not being born wealthy or being born with superior intelligence. Nor is it luck, chance or destiny. It is, however, learning and applying simple, yet proven, methods which have led millions of folks to success in the past and will continue to lead millions to success in the future. Again, there is no big secret. These principles have been around for many, many years.

The greatest thing of all about these success principles and the reason why I am where I am today is because they can be learned by anyone, anyone who is willing to learn them and apply them in their everyday lives. That's all there is to it! Honestly!

In short, you don't have to have a college degree or possess superior knowledge to become successful. That's been proven throughout history time and time again. Many of the wealthiest men and women in the world never went to college. Some of them never even made it through high school! Yet, they now control industries. To get to the top, these people all learned and applied the same success principles which were used by many others in the past. Again, there is no big secret.

One more thing. The biggest key to success in any industry is not knowledge (although knowledge is very important). It's TIMING! That's why it's imperative to choose the right industry, one that's on its way up - not down. In my opinion, that industry is Network Marketing.

No rule of

success

will work if

you

don't make it work.

2

The Industry to Be in

Knowing how much this country has changed over the past 20 years, wouldn't it be tragic if there was no way out of this mess? That's why I am so thankful for this industry. It truly does offer a way out. In my opinion, I believe Network Marketing was sent down from God in heaven, as a silver lining behind a dark cloud. The dark cloud, of course, is this country's financial instability. I can state with confidence that Network Marketing was the escape for me and many, many others. It can be your escape too!

How can ordinary people build something for themselves, when everything appears to be falling apart? The answer is to get involved in an industry that is on its way up. On its way up doesn't mean one good year. It means steady growth year after year. This sounds like Network Marketing to me. Don't get me wrong, Network Marketing isn't the only industry on its way up. There are others. But do you have the education, the money or the connections to get involved with those other industries? When I first started, I didn't.

Prior to Network Marketing

I want you to realize I was not born with a silver spoon in my mouth. Far from it! I was born in Philadelphia, Pa. I come from a family of 6 children. Growing up, we lived in a three-bedroom row home. The sleeping arrangements were as follows: Mom and Dad occupied one bedroom. My sister had her own room. And I shared my bedroom with my 4 brothers. We had 2 sets of bunk beds in our room, and my youngest brother Brian (by choice) slept on the floor.

This is a very common living situation in Philadelphia. Now, I'm sure if you lived in a single home your whole life, you may be feeling a bit claustrophobic by reading this. But, I have no regrets. It sure was a lot of fun growing up there.

Looking back, however, no one in my neighborhood ever talked about becoming successful. We all figured success just wasn't meant for us. We were taught to get a good job with benefits and to work real hard. Then, one day, we'd be able to retire on the fruits of our efforts.

This advice may have worked 20 to 40 years ago, but it no longer works today. Sadly, the friends of mine who did take this advice (which was 98% of them), are just trying to survive today. I almost settled for it myself.

Living in L.A.

When I was 20 years old, my twin brother Mike and I moved to California. This was one of the best things we ever did! We lived in Los Angeles. Out there, success was everywhere! We met movie stars, rock stars and multi-millionaires.

Living in L.A. definitely filled me with the **desire** to want to become successful. It was a totally different world. It's really amazing how people can live on the same planet, yet live totally different lifestyles.

One of my best friends in L.A. is Cissy King. Cissy used to dance on the Lawrence Welk Show. She lives in Beverly Hills. Talk about a dynamic individual. The first time I ever went to her house, I just couldn't believe it! The view from her backyard was incredible. I stared in awe for hours. She was successful, and it showed. I learned so many valuable things from her in such a short period of time.

Anyway, the reason for me sharing this story with you is we will only become successful in this industry when we have the **desire** to want to do so. For me, getting to see success firsthand, like I saw with Cissy, made me want success too! It gave me something to shoot for.

At first, I have to admit, it was a real culture shock for me. Because as I mentioned earlier, I was used to living in a row home. After awhile, however, I got real used to it. This **desire** did not make me wealthy, but it did send signals to my brain telling me that I wanted to become successful.

Then, when I was finally introduced to Network Marketing four years later, I felt that same desire I felt back in 1985 (when I was living in L.A.). This feeling overwhelmed me! I knew this was it! I knew I had finally found the industry that would show me the right way, if I was willing to work hard and believe in myself.

Once you know "**why**" you're building your business, you'll have that same burning desire I had. And believe me, no one will be able to stop you either! In short, when you have something to shoot for, and it's backed with **desire - action** always follows.

A Legitimate Low Cost Business

Network Marketing offers an opportunity to anyone who is willing to work hard and believe in themselves. Like I already mentioned, you do not need a college education to become successful in this industry. Nor do you have to know people in high places. And you certainly don't need a million dollars either. In fact, Network Marketing is quite the opposite. It's a low cost, low overhead, high profit industry. I honestly don't know of any other industry like this!

To be part of a Network Marketing company as an independent distributor costs next to nothing. I mean think about it, we do not have to shell out all that money for product research, the materials, the engineers who design the products and services, a warehouse to store them in, insurance to protect the inventory, payroll for the company's employees, etc. The company you represent pays for all of that. We just pay our yearly distributorship fee, and then we're entitled to plug into an already established multi-million dollar company, where we can build a business for ourselves with little or no money out of our own pockets. Talk about awesome!

Also, we do not have to go to school for 4 years and spend thousands of dollars to learn how to do this business (like most of us do when we go to college). No, in Network Marketing, we're trained by the people who are already successful in this industry. What a concept!

In my opinion, however, it should cost a lot more money to get involved in this industry. It's too cheap! I say this because most of us take the Network Marketing concept too lightly! We do this because of the small financial commitment that is required to get started. Most of us figure $20 - $500 is no big loss to us if we don't succeed.

29

Just thinking this way will hurt you! I'll bet if this business cost $100,000 to get started, no one would take it too lightly! We couldn't afford to! Therefore, just because it's inexpensive, DO NOT TAKE IT LIGHTLY! Remember, this industry is one of the most powerful and profitable industries in the world!

When I started, I didn't take this industry too lightly. I couldn't afford to. I was dead broke! I needed this business to work for me. If it didn't, I would have lost everything I owned. I honestly couldn't even afford to pay the application fee when I first started. My upline distributor, however, told me, "If you can't afford to do this business, Patrick, you can't afford *not* to!"

At the time, I didn't quite understand what he meant, and you may not either. What he meant, however, was that if I was 25 years old, and I couldn't even afford a $30 application fee, something had to be terribly wrong with my life. He was right. Something was wrong. I was dead broke! This makes total sense to me now. Therefore, if you're struggling today, and you cannot afford to get started, you too cannot afford **not** to get started. If this is the case, you need this business more than it needs you, just like I did only a few years ago.

Network Marketing
Brings Us All Together

One of the greatest things about Network Marketing is it takes people from all walks of life and from all different backgrounds and gives us something we can all do together. When I first started, I was so excited! I closed my pizza business down immediately so I could do my Network Marketing business full time. My family thought I was nuts! On top of that, a good friend of mine, who was a licensed funeral director, and I were telling everyone we were going to become successful together doing this business. Now my family thought I was completely nuts!

My friend's name is George Hanitz. As I already mentioned, George was a licensed funeral director. I was a broke business owner. And we were going to become successful together in Network Marketing?! No one believed us. I can't say I blamed them. I mean, where can a funeral director and a broke business owner come together in business and become successful together? The answer is Network Marketing. It didn't matter that no one believed in us. *We did!* And that's all that mattered.

Network Marketing is so powerful! It really helps to reunite families, friends and relatives again. Today, most families are so busy going in different directions with their lives, they barely get to know each other. However, once they do get to work together in this great industry and actually build something together, they can get to know each other again.

I've seen so many beautiful situations where this industry has brought families back together again. I saw a father and his daughter get back together again and build a business together all over the country. I also saw a girl and her sister reunite again and actually get along. This was great because they never could get along prior to doing this business. This business is truly amazing. *It is a real miracle worker!* My question is - *How can anyone knock this industry?*

Residual Income

Any way you slice it, Network Marketing comes out ahead of the rest. Another one of the many great benefits of Network Marketing is *residual income*. What this means is, whatever product or service you sell, and whatever group you build for yourself, will not only benefit you this year, it will benefit you next year too! This goes on year after year. The only way this will end is if you quit. Now that's what I call *security!*

Does it work this way with other leading industries? For the most part, no. Let's say you sell real estate. Will whatever you sell this year, also benefit you next year? No. Next year you'll have to start all over again. How about automobile sales? Jewelry sales? Clothing? Furniture? I'm sure you get the point.

In this industry, every time you or anyone in your group sells a product or service, you get paid. Further, every time your customers use your services or order more products, you get paid all over again, whether you sold it to them or not! Why? Because if the customer likes your products and services, and they want more, they have to go through you (or the people in your group) to get them. That's because your products and services are not sold in stores. Therefore, if you're planning on building a group of distributors, (which I highly recommend you do) residual income is, and will be, a major part of your income.

Other People's Efforts

Everything you've read so far up to this point about Network Marketing has been great. However, if there is one reason I can give you above all the rest that will convince you of the power of this industry, it has to be this: You can become wealthy doing this business part time! That's right. You're not hearing things. I did say you can become successful doing this business part time. The reason? It's simple. Other people's efforts.

Example. Let's say you put 10 hours a week into your part-time business. Do you think you can find 3 people to do the same thing? Of course you can! This will give you 40 hours a week in your business. Now, out of these 40 hours, how many of them will you have worked yourself? 10. Is 10 hours a week considered part time? Sure it is!

Now, what if your 3 new distributors find 3 people each themselves, who also agree to put in 10 hours a week each? That would be 90 hours more! Add this to the 40 hours you already have. This would give you 130 hours a week. Pretty awesome, huh?

Out of these 130 hours, how many will you work yourself? 10. If you had to work the 130 hours yourself, you'd be pretty tired, wouldn't you? Further, you really wouldn't enjoy your success. That's the key. You don't have to work all those hours yourself! Everyone works together as a team!

By the way, this is an extremely small scenario. What if you have 100 distributors putting 10 hours each per week? This would give you 1,000 hours a week in your group. What if you have 200 distributors putting in 10 hours a week each? 500? 1,000? 5,000? 10,000?

This, my friends, is how you can become successful by only working part time in this business. This business is not you working 1,000 hours a week yourself. That would be impossible. This business is, however, a lot of people putting in a few hours each. This further demonstrates why average people with literally no business backgrounds are getting involved and are building high-profit businesses for themselves in such short periods of time.

That's all I did. I got involved and built a national business for myself within one year. I didn't do it because I was great. No. I did it because I had a lot of help from my friends (other people's efforts). I give all the credit for my success to the people who were in my group, this great industry and to God above. Without them, I could never have done it!

Realize this: You have in your hands an opportunity to take advantage of the greatest industry the world will ever see. This industry is not on trial. It works! The question is, are you willing to work too? This industry is producing more success stories than any other industry in the world! This business is not only putting money back in people's bank accounts, it's also putting life back in the people!

The greatest

ignorance

is to

reject something

you know nothing

about.

3

Is This a Pyramid?

Is this a pyramid? I'm sure you have all heard this question many times. When I'm asked this question, I usually reply, "What do you mean is this a pyramid?" The most popular response I get in return is, "I don't know. I just heard these things are illegal pyramid schemes." Did you ever notice the people who question things, when asked what they mean, usually have no idea what they're asking? This really blows my mind! Anyway, let's try to answer this question for you so you'll know how to handle it in the future. Fair enough?

First of all, what is a pyramid? A pyramid is a solid triangular figure which, when formed, is one of the strongest structures known to man. What is a scheme? A scheme is a plan, design or a system. Now, is Network Marketing a pyramid? No. Is Network Marketing a plan or system, that when successfully built, takes the shape of a pyramid? Absolutely!

Every Large Business is Shaped Like a Pyramid

I don't know of any large business, organization or government that isn't shaped this way! Now, there are two kinds of business-shaped pyramids - one is legal and the other is illegal. But we'll discuss that later. For now, let's see if the larger companies in this country are also shaped like pyramids.

Think of any large well known company. Who is at the very top of that company? The president, right? He/she then appoints a few key people as vice presidents. They, in turn, look for a few people to manage various regional sections of the country. These people, in turn, look for people to manage local offices in their regions. This process continues until it reaches the bottom of the pyramid. This is where the so-called *average employees or laborers* begin. Now, if you wrote this down on paper, wouldn't it take the form of a pyramid? Sure it would.

Let's take an organization. Any organization is fine. One person is appointed president of the organization, and he/she goes through the same process the president of a large corporation goes through, appointing key people until it reaches the bottom of the pyramid (where the masses are). How about the church groups?

Let's use the catholic church as an example. This pyramid starts with the Pope. Underneath the Pope are the cardinals. Then come the arch-bishops. Then the bishops, and so on. At the very bottom are the parishioners. Now, are there more parishioners or Popes? More employees or presidents? Do you see my point? They're all pyramids.

Therefore, you need to realize that pyramid-shaped businesses, groups and organizations are everywhere. As a matter of fact, I don't know of any large business that is shaped any differently. Could you imagine if there were one hundred presidents and just one employee? One billion Popes and only one parishioner? Did you ever hear the expression, "Too many Chiefs and not enough Indians?" When this happens, businesses begin to fail.

Where Does the Power Come From?

We now know that any successful business, organization or religion is shaped like a pyramid. The majority of the power, however, doesn't come from the top, it comes from the bottom. Why? Because that's where the majority of the people, employees and parishioners are.

This is where the question of legal or illegal comes up. Any pyramid, in order to be legal, has to have value flowing both *up* and *down* its structure. By this, I mean either efforts, products, services, votes, money, etc.

For example, when you work for someone, you usually put in 40 hours a week of your time. Your *effort* is the value that flows *up* the pyramid. If you're *paid* for your efforts, that would be the value which flows *down*. This would be considered a *legal pyramid*. An illegal pyramid has *no value flowing down* it. So, if a company hired you and didn't pay you for your efforts, that would be illegal.

Let's look at the churches. What value flows up this pyramid? Money. The money comes from the parishioners at the bottom of the pyramid. What value flows down this pyramid? Prayer, support, guidance, etc. Therefore, the church groups are legal pyramid structures. How about the government? What value flows up this pyramid? Tax dollars and votes. Every American tax payer pours value up this pyramid whether we want to or not. What value flows down this pyramid? That's debatable.

Is Network Marketing Legal?

In order for Network Marketing to be legal, it too has to have value flowing both *up* and *down* the pyramid. And it does! Money flows up this pyramid, and product, training and support flow down it. Therefore, Network Marketing is also a legal pyramid structure, just like IBM, G.M., and your local churches and organizations.

When you put money into the Network Marketing pyramid, you're purchasing product. Even before you purchase the product, you know exactly what you're getting in return for your money. How can that be illegal? It's like starting your own clothing business. You purchase the clothing wholesale and then sell it retail. Same thing.

Network Marketing has been around for over 50 years. This industry does billions of dollars in gross revenue sales each and every year (and is increasing at a rate of 20% - 30% annually!). If Network Marketing was an illegal pyramid, with the kind of growth we're experiencing, it would have been outlawed years ago. There is no way the U.S. government would allow any industry, including Network Marketing, to do billions of dollars annually if it was illegal! *Think about it!*

If it was considered illegal, however, a much larger problem would have immediately existed. We would rightfully have to close down all the church groups, corporate companies, organizations and governments who are structured this way. They're pyramids too, right? Could you imagine that? Who would be left standing? Not many.

Now, I'm not here to knock other industries. I just want to get the truth out about Network Marketing. A lot of people turn away from this industry because they hear certain things about it which, for the most part, are untrue. This is sad, because once you really get to know this industry, you'll have to agree that it rises above them all.

Now, I'm certainly not saying that every Network Marketing company is totally legitimate. I don't even know every Network Marketing company. So how could I make such a statement! However, there is one thing I'm absolutely positive of - *there is good and bad in everything.* Good industries - bad industries. Good companies - bad companies. Good church groups - bad church groups. Good non-profit organizations - bad non-profit organizations. Good governments - bad governments. Good Network Marketing companies - bad Network Marketing companies.

The People Make the Industry

I personally don't know any bad Network Marketing companies, but I'm sure they do exist. The reason? In my opinion, industries don't fail, people do! And I know you're aware of the fact that there are good people and bad people in every industry.

Let's take the automobile industry. What kind of reputation does this industry have? A bad one, right? Why? Because of the people. Does this mean all automobile sales people are greedy rip-off artists? Of course not! As a matter of fact, the majority of the people in that industry are good-hearted, ethical people.

These individuals just happened to enter into an industry that has had a bad reputation for many years. Because of this reputation, automobile sales people are labeled as rip-off artists, con-men, etc. The truth is, there still are some unethical automobile sales people out there. But once again, the majority of them are decent people.

Every industry has both good and bad people who either add credibility to the industry or give it a bad

40

name. This includes the insurance industry, the medical industry, the government, large corporate companies, church groups, non-profit organizations, etc. The same goes for Network Marketing.

The point I'm driving at here is, Network Marketing is the most incredible industry on the face of the earth. However, there are good and bad people in this industry too! I can honestly say that 97% of the people who are involved in this industry are the greatest people you will ever meet! This industry attracts the best of the best. However, once in a while, we're going to get someone involved who has the potential to give our industry a bad reputation. Remember - this not only happens in Network Marketing, it happens in every industry. But don't worry, they'll never stop us. We're too strong.

In closing, Network Marketing IS a legal business which, when built, is shaped like a pyramid, just like IBM, G.M., the government, all religious groups, all your local organizations, and so on. Because Network Marketing is rapidly becoming one of the world's largest industries, it is and always will be regulated.

In the U.S., Network Marketing is regulated by the Federal Trade Commission (FTC) and other agencies. Once again, if it was illegal, it would have been outlawed years ago. And it certainly wouldn't be regulated by these government agencies. Instead, it would be closed down by them! Therefore, Network Marketing (like all the other pyramid-shaped businesses), is legal as long as there is *value* flowing both *up* and *down* its structure. So let's put an end to the rumors. By the way, if a pyramid is such a bad thing, why would it be on the back of a one dollar bill?

Look

for the

good,

not the

bad.

4

Have You Ever Heard Bad Things about Network Marketing?

Here is another question which needs to be addressed. The previous question, "Is this a pyramid," is a question which usually comes from people who are not involved with this industry. The question of hearing bad things about Network Marketing, however, originates mostly from those individuals who used to be involved. Once again, it's not the industry that's bad, but some of its people.

Some people get involved and expect everything to be done for them. These people are the ones who order product and then put it underneath their beds and hope the product will grow legs and sell itself. When this doesn't happen, they begin to complain, "I knew it! I knew I was being taken for a ride. I heard about these things before. They really got me good!"

These people are the problem! They actually feel Network Marketing owes them something!

Once again, Network Marketing offers no guarantees. It's not an $8/hr. job. *It's an opportunity!* Everyone receives the same product, compensation plan and training. It's then up to the individual to make his/her opportunity work for them. This not only happens in Network Marketing, mind you. People succeed and fail in every industry! The ones who fail never blame themselves, they blame the industry. These people should never get started in the first place.

When I do my trainings, I tell the audience over and over again that there are no guarantees. Therefore, if certain individuals want guarantees, I tell them they're looking at the wrong industry. There are no guarantees out there anywhere! This business is not for whiners! It's for doers! This business will not work for you, unless you work for it! It's that simple!

Once you do commit to this business and you work hard, you'll see just how powerful this industry really is. And after you achieve some success in this industry, I know you'll agree there's no better industry out there. Further, the more success you have in this industry, the more angry you'll get with those individuals who don't even try in this business, and then cry the blues because they claim they were taken advantage of.

When I hear these ex-distributors complaining and knocking this industry, I say to myself, "Are they sure they're talking about Network Marketing, the industry that has totally changed my life and the lives of many others for the better? They must be thinking of another industry."

However, just like with anything else in life, *the ones who sow, shall reap, and the ones who don't shall go hungry.*

Let's Compare Industries

We can compare any industry you want. There's nothing even close to Network Marketing. If we made a list of the *pros* and *cons* of 10 different industries, with 1 of them being Network Marketing, I'm very confident Network Marketing would rise to the top of them all. In fact, the only con I can honestly see with Network Marketing (besides a few unethical distributors) is the people who get involved, fail, and then blame the industry.

Everything else, from the compensation plans to the products and services are the best out there. Nothing even comes close! Here's proof: Think of any industry besides Network Marketing.

Now, answer the upcoming questions as best you can on the industry you have in mind. Then, answer them on Network Marketing, o.k.?

1.) If I had to draw a graph showing the projected growth for this industry for the next 10 years, what would it look like? Will this industry even exist in 10 years?

2.) What is the percentage of people who do not have the products and services this industry offers? Is the market wide open, or does everyone already have one?

3.) What are my chances of rising up to the top of this industry? Is it even possible?

4.) Does this industry offer an opportunity to earn residual income from the people I train?

5.) Does this industry allow me to work whenever I want, with whom I want to work, and wherever I want to work?

I hope these questions further prove to you the power of this industry, and most importantly, where it's headed. The future is really bright! Wouldn't you agree?

In short, there will always be someone out there saying something bad about Network Marketing. No industry, government, church group, organization or company is free from this unfair criticism. The more success an industry has, the more the unsuccessful and jealous people will knock it. But don't worry, these people are critical about everything. They are usually lazy people who are unsuccessful in everything they do. Yet, they continue to blame the industries for their failures. *Such is life.*

Too much time

spent in complaining

leaves

too little time

for doing.

5

Why Network Marketing will Never Fail

In my opinion, Network Marketing can't fail! It's getting bigger and bigger everyday. The momentum is incredible. It's like a 747 jet airplane on the runway taking off. Who is going to stop it? No one. Now, I do admit no one can stop a 747 from falling out of the sky either! But that will never happen with Network Marketing. There are many reasons I can give you to back this statement up. Here are just a few of them.

Everyone is Getting Involved

Network Marketing is definitely the most powerful way to reach consumers in the 90's. There's no better way to get a product or service right into the consumer's hands. Experts predict that in the 90's, Network Marketing will fuse Americans from coast to coast into one gigantic, pulsating sales ameba. This is definitely happening! That's why more and more ex-C.E.O.'s, vice presidents, doctors, stockbrokers, etc., are making career changes, and joining this multi-billion dollar industry.

Fortune 500 companies are also getting involved. They are desperate to reach consumers face to face. So, by knowing where Network Marketing is headed, some of these companies have already switched, while others are seriously considering the proposition. Yes, there are still those people who will laugh at the concept and will not even consider Network Marketing. But I can promise you, in a few years, Network Marketing will have the last laugh.

It Works Everywhere

Network Marketing is, as I've already stated, a multi-billion dollar industry, and is growing at a rate of 20% - 30% each year. Network Marketing is rapidly expanding all over the world. The reason for such rapid expansion is because it offers ordinary people a legitimate opportunity to build full or part-time businesses for themselves and their families. What other industry offers this?

Network Marketing can turn a negative situation into a positive one. For instance, it offers for the victims of buy-outs, mergers and layoffs in corporate America the opportunity to plug into this unique and powerful industry. They can then use their talents and experience to build something for themselves, instead of for their former employers.

Another thing is it doesn't matter where you live! Whether it's a large city or a small town, there is a percentage of people in every geographical area who will see an opportunity. Here is an example: Let's say the percentage of people who will see an opportunity is 3% - 7%. This would mean that if you lived in a town with a population of 50,000 people, 1,500 to 3,500 of them will get involved. That's only one small town! How about a town with 100,000 people? 200,000? 1,000,000? 5,000,000?

Further, you're not limited to only your home town. You can build your business anywhere! Now, you may say that you don't know anyone outside of your hometown. That's okay too! Does someone in your group know anyone in a different town or city?

Think about it. If one of your distributors knows someone in Los Angeles, and he/she signs up, guess who now has a group in one of the largest cities in the world? Pretty neat, huh? Do you think your new L.A. distributor knows people in San Diego? San Francisco? Phoenix? Talk about awesome! You could live in a small town on the east coast. Even so, everything your new west coast distributor does benefits you too! Now, that's smart business to me.

Network Marketing is Fair to Everyone

Network Marketing is not prejudiced towards any race, sex, religion, age (usually 18 and up) or background. This is the only opportunity I know where you will truly earn what you're worth. Think about it, the products and services are the same for everyone. They don't make *blue* products for the men and *pink* ones for the women. The compensation plan is also the same for everyone. They don't pay you less because of the color of your skin or because of your sex. Women have the same pay plan as the men.

So, if the opportunity is the same for everyone, why doesn't everyone make the same amount of money? Because, it's up to the individual to generate his/her income. WHAT YOU PUT INTO YOUR BUSINESS, IS WHAT YOU'RE GOING TO GET OUT OF IT.

Is it that way in the corporate structure? No way. In corporate America, it does matter what your skin color is and what your sex, age, religion and past are. A woman will do the same job a man will do, and sometimes even better, but still earn less money. A black man may be up for a promotion, only to be passed over by a white man with much less experience. An upper management executive may be shooting for the vice president's promotion, only to be passed over by the C.E.O.'s son, who just graduated from college and is still wet behind the ears.

Face it, most promotions in corporate America, and the world, for that matter, are unfair. They come mostly to those who brown nose the company and its leadership, stab anyone and everyone in the back to get the promotion, and who are willing to work 80 hours a week.

In Network Marketing, however, to get promoted you have to work. No brown nosing the company; no back stabbing; just hard work. And in order for your people to get promoted, you need to help them. By helping them, you help yourself. The more you help them, the more income you'll earn. It's that simple.

It Just Makes Sense

Another reason why Network Marketing will never fail is that it just makes sense. J. Paul Getty once quoted, "I'd rather earn 1% on the efforts of 100 people, rather than 100% of my own efforts." He also said, "In order for any industry to succeed, it needs to have a product or service that nobody has, everyone needs, is priced for sale, and is priced for profit." He then concluded, "The key to any business explosion is timing."

That's why Network Marketing makes so much sense. It ties in perfectly with what Mr. Getty said. We do earn money from other people's efforts. We do offer products and services that nobody has, but will have in the future. These products and services are priced for sale and for profit. The key factor, of course, is *timing*. This is where we outshine everyone else. You couldn't pick a better time to get involved like right now.

There is Hope

In my opinion, however, the biggest reason why Network Marketing will never fail is because every human being has a small *flame* inside us called *hope*. This light is inside every one of us; whether we are a person on welfare, a laid off executive or a disabled veteran. *This light never goes out!* It may diminish at times; but it never goes out. As long as there is an opportunity (hope) and a proven path to run on, this inner light can be fueled until it becomes an inner blaze.

Network Marketing offers hope to anyone who is willing to commit to this industry and believe in themselves. It doesn't matter where you live. There are people all throughout your area who are in search of a better life. Network Marketing will be the answer for many of these people.

It offers an opportunity for ordinary people to have extra ordinary lifestyles in a short period of time. Of course, there are no guarantees. Once again, *what you put into it is what you're going to get out of it.* But there is *hope*, and with that, *anything* is possible.

Don't sit back

and take what

comes.

Go after

what you want.

6

The Game of Life

I hope you are enjoying the game of life. My question to you is, are you a player or a spectator? Fact is, most of us are spectators. We sit at home and watch television all day long as if we have our whole lives ahead of us. Face it, everyday we wake up, we are one day closer to the end. We don't have all the time in the world to do the things we've always dreamed of doing. The clock is ticking. *The time is NOW!*

We were not created to be spectators in the game of life, we were created to be players. If this is the case, why are over 95% of the people in the world sitting in the bleachers, cheering for their heroes, when they should become heroes themselves? Instead of going for their dreams, they take the easy way out. I truly believe people give up too early in life! This is very sad. Face it, *you still have life in you!* My advice is, live it well.

Most of us, however, overlook this advice and accept the role of being spectators. The amazing thing about the spectators is they are always so critical of the players. They feel the players owe them something! The spectators, who do little or nothing with their lives, expect the players to be perfect. They are always telling the players how it should be done. Now, if they really knew, wouldn't they be on the field playing, instead of sitting in the bleachers? This blows my mind! They criticize everyone.

For instance, let's take a professional athlete. He works real hard his whole life and beats enormous odds before he can actually make it. In a sense, he is one in a million. Then, when he finally does make it, the spectators expect him to be perfect. If he is a quarterback in the NFL, the spectators expect him to complete every pass. If he doesn't, he will have 60,000+ fans booing him and even threatening him.

The bottom line is, who is the one on the field playing? The player. He is the one who worked 7 days a week, 18 hours a day to get where he is today. Who are the ones in the bleachers? The spectators. The spectators feel they have the right to say whatever they want to the player, because they are helping to pay his salary. That's absurd! That's like saying, if you work for the city or state, I can call you whatever I want to because I am helping to pay your salary. It's the same thing.

The reason why the player has 60,000+ fans watching him play every week is because he did whatever it took to get there. He decided to go for it; to be a player in life. Don't get me wrong, some of the spectators at the game are also players, but on a different field. The majority, however, merely exist.

What is a player? *A player is someone who goes for his/her dreams and continues, despite opposition.* Whether they actually get as far as they would like is not important. What is important, however, is that they are playing. They realize - *the biggest risk in life is not risking.* Players also realize if they don't go for their dreams, they'll regret it the rest of their lives.

Joseph Campbell, the great mythologist put it this way:

"But if a person has had the sense of the Call - the feeling that there's an adventure for him, and if he doesn't follow that but remains in the society because it's safe and

secure, then life dries up. And then he comes to that condition in late middle age; he's gotten to the top of the ladder, and found that it's against the wrong wall......."

"If you have the guts to follow the risk, however, life opens, opens, opens up along the line. I feel that if one follows what I call one's bliss - the thing that really gets you deep in the gut and that you feel is your life - doors will open up. They do! They have in my life and they have in many lives that I know of."

Folks, when it comes to the game of life, the players always win and the spectators always lose. Even when the players fail from time to time, they still win because at least they are participating. Of course, when they do fail from time to time, they're disappointed, but not as disappointed as they'd be if they never tried. Then, they'd be doomed to a life of misery.

One of the saddest things I have ever seen is the player who, after a failure or two, decides he/she is not worth the very best in life and joins the spectators in the stands. Talk about regression! The saddest thing is, a lot of these ex-players in life quit just one step away from real success.

Fact is, most of us use only a small percentage of our potential. This is because most of us are not doing what we want to do with our lives. How can you use all of your potential, when you don't even enjoy what you're doing? You can't. I don't believe a person should work a job he/she doesn't like. If this is you, it's not too late to change. I did, therefore, you can too!

Most people are too afraid to go for their dreams. Although the reasons are many, the end result is always the same - a life of unhappiness. Think about this: Most people are afraid to go for their dreams because they're afraid of going broke in the process. Isn't it funny how most of them are broke anyway without even trying? I don't get it! My motto is: *I'd rather have nothing to live on and something to live for than to have something to live on and nothing to live for.*

Where does Network Marketing fit in all of this? It's simple. Network Marketing is a vehicle which helps a lot of ordinary people, like myself, achieve high levels of success. We can then afford to do what we really want to do with the rest of our lives. Network Marketing was not a career choice I made as a kid growing up. I'll bet there is not one person who planned to be involved in Network Marketing prior to starting. After seeing its power, however, it was obvious there was a serious opportunity for anyone who wanted it.

That's why Network Marketing is as big as it is today. People get involved for various reasons. Most people, however, get involved because they know they can work hard for 3 years and earn the kind of money they need to take their lives up to the next level.

There are many C.E.O.'s of large companies today who made their first fortunes in Network Marketing. Even today, these people are earning checks from their Network Marketing businesses. Not too bad, huh?

On the other hand, there are so many people who are dead broke and unhappy with their lives. Even so, they won't quit their jobs and go for their dreams. These people imprison themselves to a life of failure. *The prison walls they build are only limits they place upon themselves. In reality, they're not walls, they're only negative thoughts which can be built higher or destroyed upon its master's command.* If we lack in life, it's because we think in lack.

57

In closing, if you are building your Network Marketing business with a **Purpose** in mind, then you, my friend, are a player in life. We all heard the expression, *"You only go around once."* My advice is, listen to these words and live your life by them.

By being a player, the only one you have to impress by going for your dreams is *yourself*. On the other hand, the only one who will be disappointed if you don't go for your dreams is also *yourself*. For me, when it comes to the game of life, not even tickets on the 50 yard line will suffice. I need to be a player. How about you? Are you a *player* in life? Or a *spectator*?

You're only

young

once.

Do It Now!

Part Two

The Things
You
Must Do
for
Success

You can pay

the price for

success

or you will pay

the price of

failure.

7

Whatever it Takes

I have been training the Network Marketing industry for over 5 years now. During this time, I've come to realize a few things. First, everyone who gets involved in this industry wants to become successful. Second, there are certain things you must be willing to do in order to become successful. And third, few of us are willing to do them.

Sadly, this not only happens in Network Marketing. Think about it, in every industry throughout America (and the world), there are certain things which must be done in order to become successful. And like Network Marketing, everyone involved in those industries also want to become successful, but again few are willing to do what it takes.

This used to blow my mind! Now it makes total sense to me. Most people are just not serious. And until they get serious, success will avoid them like the plague. In the end, folks, we have either *reasons* or *results*.

Those of us who are not where we want to be in life (which is most of us), usually have reasons or excuses to justify our existences. We can say that he or she took advantage of us, and that's why we failed; or so and so led us down the wrong path. But in the end, although they are good reasons, they won't help us become successful.

When we blame others for the things that happen to us in life, we become victims. When this happens, we lose control, and we become powerless from stopping others from doing the same thing to us in the future. However, once we realize the fact that we *did* have something to do with where we are today in life, we become responsible. We then gain control back.

Face it, no one likes to blame themselves for anything. The ones who do, however, are the ones who are in control of themselves. And by being in control, they can avoid negative situations from happening to them again in the future. That's what all the real leaders do. They are the ones who get positive results in life.

Something to Think About

What if you got involved in Network Marketing, started part time, and after 3 months with little or no success, you decided this business was not for you. Would it be the end of the world? Of course not! You'd probably still have your full-time job, and you'd continue to do what you did in the past.

On the other hand, let's say you got involved, started part time, and you faithfully used this training. After seeing immediate results, you started to share your opportunity with other people. Three months later, you had 5-10 part-time distributors in your downline who also started duplicating this training. How would you feel?

Two months later, after applying the same principles, you signed up 5-10 more part-time distributors, and so did the people in your group! How would you feel now? Would you quit? No, of course not! You would be extremely excited! Most importantly, you would be motivated to continue building your part-time business.

In the upcoming months, you kept repeating this very simple process over and over again. Within a year, using only your part-time profits, you bought a brand new vehicle. You also realized you were earning more money with your part-time business than you were with your full-time job, and your part-time income was increasing monthly! Further, you're having more fun, you're helping a lot of people, and most importantly, you are your own boss.

Now, back to reality.

How would you feel about your full-time job now? You know, the place where you're told day after day from your boss what to do, what to say, when to work, when to leave, and most importantly, how much you're worth! Talk about sad! At this point, I'm sure you would realize the fact that you have been wasting your whole life literally sacrificing yourself for your boss and the company. On top of that, you were underpaid to do so. *Imagine that!*

That's when you would realize it's time for a change. It would now be time for you to fire your boss and turn your part-time business into your full-time career. From this day on, you would be the boss. You would be in control. You would call the shots. In other words, you would no longer be making a living, you would be living a lifestyle. What an unbelievable feeling!

Now, if you've already reached this goal with your Network Marketing business, or even surpassed it, you can relate to the incredible feeling I've just described. That's because you did whatever it took to get these results.

However, if you're new, part time or never had the proper training, this is still just a dream to you. But don't be discouraged! *This is America!* The place where *dreams* can come true!

However, in order for it to happen, you need to be willing to do *whatever it takes* for its attainment. This includes taking responsibility for *everything* that has happened to you in the past, whether it's good or bad. That's what the next chapter is all about. We're going to break down the **10** things you **must** be willing to do in order to get to the top of this industry. Fair enough? Good! Let's get busy!

The person who

wants to do

something

finds a way;

the other kind finds

an excuse.

8

The "Whatever it Takes" List

Over the past couple of years, I have come up with a list of things we must do in order to become successful in Network Marketing. I call this list my *"Whatever it Takes"* list. This list is very simplistic. However, don't let its simplicity fool you. These things **must** be done in order to achieve success on a massive scale.

Every successful person in this industry naturally does all the things I am about to share with you. When I say successful people, I am not talking about the ones who are earning $40,000 or $50,000 a year. I am speaking of the ones who are earning $400,000 or $500,000 a year and more! Where do you want to be?

Of course, if you master 50% of this list, you'll still achieve a great deal of success. Even if you master only 10% of it, you'll still achieve some success, but you'll never get to the top! Therefore, if you want to get to the *top* of this industry, I recommend you master the whole thing. It goes as follows:

1.) You need to realize success *can* happen to you. You can be dead broke today, it doesn't matter. As long as you are willing to do *whatever it takes* to become successful, you'll eventually get there. It all starts in the mind. Success comes to those who are success conscious, and failure comes to those who are failure conscious.

Again, most of us have been taught and trained to be average. It doesn't, however, have to be that way! There are millions of successful people all over the world who started where you are right now. They never gave up. You can't either! If they can do it, you can too! However, you cannot command success, you must deserve it.

Further, there are no laws which ban you from becoming successful, unless you create them yourself. Think about it, you can look in any law book, in any language, in any country around the world, and I guarantee you will not find one line in any of those books which prohibits you legally from becoming successful.

On top of that, you are one in a billion. No one ever was, is, or ever will be exactly like you. When you were born, you were given total control over your destiny. Therefore, you need to choose the right destination. Remember, whatever course you choose, you will have to live with it for the rest of your life.

2.) You need to accept your current situation, whether it's good or bad. Acceptance is the first step towards taking action. If you don't fully accept the situation you're in right now, it will be very difficult for you to change it. However, once you do accept it (not settle for), you can move on. Face it, all the things you've done and everything that's happened to you in the past can't be changed. So you might as well just accept them.

If you're always bothered by your past, you just haven't accepted it yet. However, once you do accept it, you still may not be happy with it, but you will be able to think more clearly, and you will feel more at peace with yourself. Once again, *you can't change your past, but you can change your future.* The next time you're feeling overwhelmed with a situation, ask yourself, "What am I not accepting about this?" Then accept it and move on. You are greater than anything that can happen to you.

3.) You need to have clearly defined, yet attainable goals. All successful people have clearly defined goals. They realize goal setting is an absolute must for success. Sadly, less than 5% of the people in the world actually write their goals down. By the way, this elite group of people is worth more than the other 95% combined.

If you want to keep on getting what you're getting out of life, keep doing what you're doing. However, if you want things to change, YOU must change. If you don't change, don't expect your situation to either. Goal setting is the first step towards getting what you want out of life. I know for a fact that goal setting is *key* for success. The first 25 years of my life were lived without goals. Needless to say, my life went around in circles.

However, once I did start setting goals and writing them down, I started attaining every one of them. How can you attain something if you don't know what it is you want? The answer is - you can't. The bottom line is - you have to have something to shoot for in order to become successful in this business. This holds true in any business, for that matter. (More on goal setting later in this book.)

4.) You need to realize your attitude will determine the level of success you will achieve in this business. A lot of people say, "Give me the pay check first, and I'll have a good attitude." Who wouldn't? Truth is, your attitude comes before your paycheck. If your attitude is bad, expect a bad paycheck. If your attitude is okay, expect an okay paycheck. If your attitude is good, expect a good paycheck; and if your attitude is great, expect a great paycheck. It's that simple.

Once you choose the proper attitude, you must close your mind off to any negativity that could hurt you and your business. You should not associate with negative people who will only try to bring you down. *You are who you surround yourself with.* Therefore, you should surround yourself only with the people who will help you become successful in this business.

5.) You need to have total faith and belief in yourself, Network Marketing, your Network Marketing company, and the products and services you represent. A lot of people get involved and only have part-time faith and belief, and then they wonder why they fail. Fact is, even if you're working your business part time, you still need to have full-time faith and belief in yourself and in this industry.

Think about it, how can you have total faith and belief in yourself and this industry and not have a great attitude? The answer is - you can't. Believing in yourself doesn't mean to develop a huge ego. All it means is to believe you can succeed. Your belief or lack of belief will be seen, felt and heard clearly by your new distributors. The stronger your faith and belief is, the stronger your new distributors' faith and belief will be. Hence, your positive faith and belief will help empower them to set up a strong foundation on which to grow.

6.) You need to realize training is the absolute key to your success. We all need constant training to achieve and maintain success. With this fact in mind, my advice is to make sure the person/s who are training you know what they're doing. If you're not being trained properly, how can you possibly expect to train the people in your group properly? You can't! Fact is, without proper training, you just may train them to fail.

We all learn through repetition. It's impossible to retain everything we hear the first time it's told. Successful people realize this. That's why they are constantly learning. They are always reading books, listening to tapes and attending training seminars. I personally feel all companies should invest a percentage of their profits each year into training. Training is definitely the best investment any company or individual can make.

How will you know you're being trained properly? By the results you achieve. It's that simple! The bottom line is, the better your training, the better your results will be. Knowing this, I recommend (so that you don't risk your success and the success of the people in your group) you get the very best training you can find.

7.) You need to realize you're going to make mistakes. No one is perfect! We all make mistakes! Accept this fact! The key thing here is to learn from them. The difference between the successful and the mediocre is that successful people learn from their mistakes, while the rest of us don't. Successful people realize mistakes are only good for us when we learn from them.

Every time successful people make a mistake, they learn another way not to do it. They then fix the mistake and continue to build their dreams. The key to learning from our mistakes is not to look where we **fell**, but where we **slipped**. Remember, the person who gets things done makes many mistakes. But he/she never makes the biggest mistake of all - *doing nothing*.

When we were kids growing up, we were always punished when we made a mistake. And when we went to school, the same thing happened. There, we were expected to get A's on every test. If we didn't, we were told we'd be failures in life. Some people say, "Yeah, but that was when we were kids." Not really. What's the first thing you do when you make a mistake on the job? You look around to make sure your boss didn't see you, right? Talk about unwanted pressure! *That's ridiculous!* *Expect mistakes. Make mistakes. Learn from your mistakes.*

8.) You need to persist until you end up where you want to be. As you know, Henry Aaron is the home run king of the world. Did you know he struck out many more times than he homered? He could have easily quit after he first struck out and said, "I knew I couldn't do it!" But he didn't. Instead, he set his goal (to be the home run king), and he persisted until he finally ended up at the top.

William James, the great American psychologist, stated that we all have a psychological barrier inside us called the first layer of fatigue. "Beyond this barrier," he said, "lies tremendous power and energy." The ones who do great things break through this barrier. Persistence plays a major role in helping us to break through.

To succeed in life takes many steps in the right direction. Sometimes the road will be bumpy. Therefore, you will need to persist when those inescapable bad days come. This is why you have to know **why** you are building your business. When you do know **why**, you'll definitely have the strength you need to carry on through the rough days.

9.) You need to realize that if it's got to get done - YOU MUST DO IT! Network Marketing allows us to capitalize off of other people's efforts. This is an incredible benefit. However, it tends to make some of us lazy. I know this personally, because it paralyzed me for a short period of time. To avoid this dilemma from happening to you, my advice is - *no matter how much money you are making, you* *should always work your business like you did in the beginning.*

In other words, don't wait for the people in your group to do their share before you do yours. This will only lead you to failure. *If you want something to happen, make it happen yourself.* When you wait for the people in your group to take action on your part, you will lose control over your destiny, and you'll eventually go broke.

Nothing you read in this book will help you succeed until *personal action* is applied. The more you have on the line, the more it's up to you to make things happen yourself! So, when it's fourth and goal on the three yard line, with 5 seconds left, are you going to hand the ball off to someone else, or are you going to carry it in yourself? I certainly hope you choose the latter.

10.) You need to duplicate this training with your group. The people in your group are not going to listen to what you say, they're going to do what you do. If you're being trained properly, and you share it with the people in your group, they will also be trained properly. This is called *positive duplication.* On the other hand, if you're being trained by a not so good source, the people in your group will duplicate this training too! This, of course, is called *negative duplication.*

With this in mind, it is imperative for you to get the very best training you can get. Then, let your group duplicate it. Again, if you're going to put your faith into anyone for your training, make sure he/she knows what they're talking about. I can state with confidence that everything in this book works and should be duplicated by both you and your group.

If this training helps you (which I know it will), don't you think it will help the people in your group also? Once again, *training is the absolute key for your success in this business.* If you were a boxer, you would want the best trainer, right? Well then, you should have that same attitude when it comes to this business. In short, your group *will* duplicate everything you do. My advice is - have them duplicate this training. It will work wonders for both you and them.

Well, there you have it. The "Whatever It Takes" list of things you must do in order to achieve massive success in this industry. Once again, they are:

1.) You need to realize success *can* happen to you.

2.) You need to *accept* your current situation whether it's good or bad, and then move on.

3.) You need to have *clearly defined,* yet *attainable goals.*

4.) You need to realize your *attitude* will determine the level of success you'll achieve in this business.

5.) You need to have *total faith* and belief in yourself, Network Marketing, your Network Marketing company, and the products and services you represent.

6.) You need to realize *training* is the *key* to your success, and then commit to getting the best you can find.

7.) You need to *learn* from your mistakes.

8.) You need to *persist* until you end up where you want to be.

9.) You need to realize that if it's got to get done - *YOU MUST DO IT!*

10.) You need to *duplicate this training* with the people in your group.

As I mentioned earlier, this list is fairly simplistic. Not easy, but simple. In order for this list to work for you, you must be willing to do three things.

Realize this list to be true.

Believe in your heart you can do these things.

Do it!

One more thing. Everything you do in this business should be done ethically. Nothing should be done unless everyone involved benefits from it. *I truly believe that everything you do in life comes back to you.* If you are working your business in an unethical way, I can promise you, sooner or later, it will come back to haunt you. Do this business right. You will not regret it! I promise you!

Do I really want to become successful in Network Marketing? *Why?*

Am I willing to do *"whatever it takes"* for success?

Am I being honest with myself in answering these questions?

Nothing

will happen

until you

take the first step.

9

Goal Setting

Henry Ford once quoted, "Whether you think you can or you think you can't, you're right!" I totally agree. Now, how does this quote apply to goal setting? That's simple. If you think you can set goals and become successful in this industry, you're right. And if you think you can't, again, you're right.

Every human achievement started out with a single thought, a thought that was backed by a plan, and then action. This was no exception for Henry Ford. His success also started out with a thought - to build automobiles. He then made a plan and backed his plan with action. And look what he built! The same goes for you. Once the plan is made, however, you need to totally commit to it. By committing to your plans, you are committing to yourself.

Did you ever notice we were taught everything we needed to learn in school, except how to set goals and become successful? This is sad, but true. The saddest thing about this is, if we don't plan our futures, how can we possibly know where we're going to end up?

Most of us will spend weeks and months planning our vacations and parties, but will not spend an hour or two planning our futures. The bottom line is, those who take the time to plan their future will have a good future, and those who don't - won't.

You will never work your business like you should, until you have goals to shoot for. Most people, however, get involved, but don't know *why* they want to do this business. It's almost impossible for these people to succeed. How can they? They don't even know why they're involved! Until we know *why* we're doing this business (have goals), we'll never succeed.

Now, there are many reasons why most of us don't set goals. Here are 5 reasons why;

1.) *Don't know how* - Like I said earlier, we were not taught how to set goals in school. Further, only 5% of us are ever taught how to after leaving school. Once again, sad but true.

2.) *Don't understand the importance of goals* - Most of us just don't know any better. We were brought up in homes where goal setting didn't exist. Instead of planning our futures, (setting goals) we allow someone else to plan it for us.

3.) *Not serious* - Let's face it, until we're serious with this business, little or nothing will happen. People who don't take the time to set goals are usually not serious. Unfortunately, this is the majority of us.

4.) *Fear of criticism* - Most of us fear talking about our goals with our family members and friends because we're afraid of being criticized. If this is you, my advice is, don't tell them! Only share your goals with the people who you know will support them. Remember, it's not important what others think of your goals, only what you think.

5.) *Fear of failure* - This is the greatest obstacle for success. Setting goals won't guarantee success, but it will definitely help. Once you set your goals, and you believe you can achieve them, you'll be driven from within. When that happens, no one or nothing can stop you. Clearly, it all starts with you setting your goals.

Goal setting is rather simple. All you need to do is:

Set Your Goal

Make Your Plan

Work Your Plan

When setting your goals, it's very important to know what you want to achieve long term. That's what the next segment is all about.

Let's pretend I just gave you 10 Dream Dollars. The money is to be used to buy back your dreams. Each dream will cost you one Dream Dollar. In other words, for each Dream Dollar you give back to me, I will give you one of your dreams. What 10 dreams (goals) would you pick and why?

Below are 10 Dream Dollar bills. Inside the dollar bills, write down the 10 biggest goals you want to achieve long term from doing this business and why you want these things.

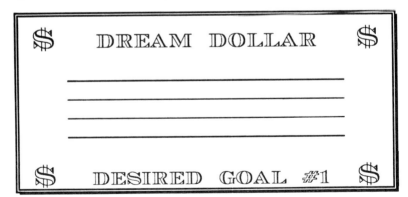

$ DREAM DOLLAR $

_____
_____
_____
_____

$ DESIRED GOAL #2 $

$ DREAM DOLLAR $

_____
_____
_____
_____

$ DESIRED GOAL #3 $

$ DREAM DOLLAR $

_____
_____
_____
_____

$ DESIRED GOAL #4 $

$ DREAM DOLLAR $

_____

$ DESIRED GOAL #5 $

$ DREAM DOLLAR $

_____

$ DESIRED GOAL #6 $

$ DREAM DOLLAR $

_____

$ DESIRED GOAL #7 $

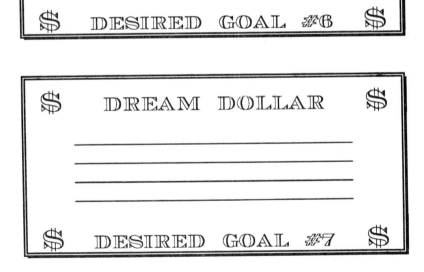

$ DREAM DOLLAR $

_____
_____
_____
_____

$ DESIRED GOAL #8 $

$ DREAM DOLLAR $

_____
_____
_____
_____

$ DESIRED GOAL #9 $

$ DREAM DOLLAR $

_____
_____
_____
_____

$ DESIRED GOAL #10 $

Now you should have a pretty good idea as to what your 10 big goals for the future are. These goals should be known as your 10 *"biggie"* goals. They should take you quite some time before you actually attain them (if not, you may not be thinking big enough). Even so, it's still important for you to know these goals upfront. Why? Because once you achieve your short term goals (which we'll discuss next), if you have no long-term **BIG** goals to shoot for, you'll get bored. You'll feel this way because there will be nothing left for you to strive for.

Besides, the greatest thrill in life is not *getting* what you want, (although this is a great feeling) it's *going* for what you want. For instance, did you ever want to go out with someone so badly, that you did whatever it took to get him/her, and after succeeding, you found out you didn't want him/her after all? That's because it was the challenge that excited you the most, not the achievement.

That's why you need to have long-term goals, so you always have something to shoot for. Besides, your 10 *"biggie"* goals are your lifetime dreams, right? Once you commit to going for your dreams, you will persevere until you get there. That is, if you're serious.

Decide

what you want.

Make a plan.

Go for it!

10

Personal Inventory List

1.) List seven things I need more of in my life.

_____
_____
_____
_____
_____
_____
_____

2.) List seven things I need less of in my life.

_____
_____
_____
_____
_____
_____
_____

3.) The top achievers in the world possess certain characteristics not found in average people. (List 10)

_____   _____
_____   _____
_____   _____
_____   _____
_____   _____

4.) In order to achieve the level of success I desire in life, I must be willing to: (List 5)

_____
_____
_____
_____
_____

5.) What would I do with my life if I knew I couldn't fail?

_____
_____
_____
_____
_____

6.) Can I see myself a millionaire?   What do I see? (Be   specific)

_____
_____
_____
_____
_____

7.) Do I deserve to be a millionaire?   Why or why not?

_____
_____
_____
_____
_____

The

purpose of life

is

a life of purpose.

11

Planning for the Future

---

5 Years From Now...

What will my net worth be?

How many people will be in my group?

What will I be driving?

Where will I be living?

Which of my closest family members and friends will be in my group?

3 Years From Now...

What will my net worth be?

How many people will be in my group?

What will I be driving?

Where will I be living?

Which of my closest family members and friends will be in my group?

1 Year From Now...

What will my net worth be?

How many people will be in my group?

What will I be driving?

Where will I be living?

Which of my closest family members and friends will be in my group?

6 Months From Now...

What will my net worth be?

How many people will be in my group?

What will I be driving?

Where will I be living?

Which of my family members and friends will be in my group?

Now that you know where you want to be in 5 years, it's very important for you to answer this question:

* Can I achieve everything I want in the future with Network Marketing?

If your answer to this question is *"Yes,"* you should consider yourself very lucky. Do you know how many people are out there who have great attitudes and big dreams, but are involved in the wrong industries? These people are dying with their music still in them. It's not their fault. Only 5% of the people in the world actually have the chance to make their dreams come true. If you answered *"yes"* to the above question, I am happy to tell you that you are one of them. Congratulations!

You now know *what* you want to achieve and *why* you're building your Network Marketing business. By knowing this, you're more than half way there. However, it's now time to talk about *what* you have to do in order to achieve your long-term goals. It's now time to talk about your monthly, weekly and daily goals. These are the most important goals for you to achieve. That's because they are the things you *have to do* in order to achieve your long-term goals. Shall we?

The greatest pleasure

in life

is doing what people say

you cannot do.

12

Monthly Goals

These goals are *key* because they'll give you the opportunity to chart your progress on a monthly basis. When setting your monthly goals, they should be big, but not so big that they're unattainable in a 30-day period. Further, these goals don't all have to be material goals. In other words, whatever you're looking to attain (whether it be recruiting a family member into your group, a promotion, a new suit, etc.), is what you should write down. Remember, they're your goals, no one else's.

You *must* specify every detail, color, shape and model of your goals. If, at month's end, you do not attain all 4 goals, don't be disappointed. It's going to take time. However, keep track of your progress from month to month. As your percentages of achievement increase, so will the smiles on your face. *It's a real exciting feeling!*

On the next page, write down the 4 major goals you want to achieve for this month. Besides writing them down, there is added space so you can clearly define them.

Do not rush this project. Take all the time you need. By the way, this project should be done each and every month. Now, turn the page and let's get busy. Once again, they're your goals. Therefore, write down what YOU want, not what other people want you to have.

Monthly Goal #1 Defined

_____
_____
_____
_____
_____
_____

Monthly Goal #2 Defined

_____
_____
_____
_____
_____

Monthly Goal #3 Defined

_____
_____
_____
_____
_____

Monthly Goal #4 Defined

_____
_____
_____
_____
_____

It's the aim that counts.

Failure to hit the

bull's eye

is never the fault

of the target.

13

Weekly Goals

This segment is very important. Therefore, it's important that when you fill in the spaces below, make sure the numbers you write down are attainable. Don't fill in large numbers to impress others. This will hurt you more than help you. On the other hand, don't write down numbers that are so small, there is no challenge to it. You want to write down numbers you really feel, that with a lot of effort, you can reach. Therefore, take time to think about them first. Remember, this is for your future. Do not take it too lightly.

1.) I **must** put at least _____ **hours** into my business each week.

2.) I **must** share the opportunity with at least _____ **people** weekly.

3.) I **must** earn at least $ _____ in **retail profits** each week.

4.) I **must** distribute at least _____ **videos** each week.

5.) I **must** attend or conduct at least _____ business opportunity **presentations** each week.

6.) I **must** give out at least _____ **free samples** (if possible) each week.

7.) **I must act professional** at all times while promoting my business.

8.) **I must read** and **listen** to my training materials every day. This will help me maintain the proper attitude and direction I need for success.

9.) **I must** be **thankful** everyday for this incredible business and constantly **support** my group in any way possible. After all, they are the biggest part of my success.

10.) **I must duplicate** these *"I must"* principles with the people in my downline.

Every man

is the architect

of his own

future.

14

Daily Goals

"Things To Do Today"

1)
2)
3)
4)   G E T   I N !
5)   G E T   I T   D O N E !
6)   G E T   O U T !
7)
8)
9)
10)

Of all the goals you need to set, your daily goals are definitely the most important. You will never get what you want in the future if you are not setting daily goals. Successful people realize this. That's why they are masters at planning 24-hour periods of time. In other words - daily goals.

Setting daily goals is simple. All you have to do is make a "Things to do today" list and accomplish everything on it. When making this list, you should only put the things on it which will pertain to your business and your personal growth. If you have other things to do which do not pertain to business, make another list. Your business list, however, should be your top priority.

Most of us have heard of making a daily list of things to do, and some of us have even experimented with it. However, hearing about it and experimenting with it will not make you wealthy. But making your list everyday and accomplishing everything on it will! Not after 1 day or 1 week, of course. But in time, the results will amaze you.

Most people, when making their list, start off with 10 things to do. That's what I recommend you do also. You can always increase or decrease it later.

Make sure, however, that you put the most important things at the very top of your list. Why? Because 20% of the things on your "Things To Do Today" list will produce 80% of your results, and the other 80% of the things will produce only 20% of your results. Therefore, it's imperative for you to do the most important things first!

Now, after making your list, why would you want to spend all day accomplishing everything on it? Most people feel they shouldn't accomplish everything on their list before 5:00 p.m., for if they do, they didn't work hard for that day. This is not true! Yes, you do want to finish everything on your list, but if you can do it in 3 hours instead of 8, why prolong it? Once you understand the "Three Get Rule" (Get In, Get It Done, Get Out), you'll want to finish your list quickly and then enjoy the rest of your life.

Question: *Why do successful people always have the time to do the real important things in life (e.g. golf, vacation, spend time with their families)?* Two reasons:

1)   Because they can.
2)   They are masters of time management.

Successful people master the "Three Get Rule" (Get In, Get It Done, Get Out). They do in 2 hours what it takes most of us 8 hours to do. They get into the office (Get in), they do everything on their list as quickly and efficiently as possible (Get It Done), and they leave (Get Out)!

That's what I call effective use of one's time! That's the main reason why they always seem to have extra time for personal matters. It's not that they don't have work to get done. That's absurd. They just seem to accomplish so much in such short periods of time. Hence, it frees up the rest of their day. That's why golfing at 1:00 p.m. is rarely out of the question for them.

You can have the same freedom also! However, you need to start **NOW!** Make tomorrow's list tonight before you go to bed. Then, when you wake up in the morning, you'll be prepared. Once you get started, your list has to be your top priority. Therefore, you'll need to focus on it. Your day shouldn't be finished until your list is.

If for some reason, however, you can't complete everything on your list due to an emergency, illness, etc., at least do the most important things. This way, even on a shortened day, you'll still achieve 80% of your results. Think about it, even on a bad day, you'll still do more than most people will do in a full day's work. What a concept! Now, if you want this to become a positive factor in your life, you'll need to be consistent. Believe me, when done right, the "Three Get Rule" will NEVER let you down. Try it.

The top is reached

by topping

yesterday's efforts.

15

Efforts vs. Results

A common question I'm asked while doing seminars is, "I'm working real hard and putting a lot of effort into my business. Why am I not getting any results?" "Well, first of all," I'll reply, "you are getting results. Everyone gets results regardless of what they do." Then I would add, "Anytime you put forth an effort, you're always going to get a result."

The same holds true for you too! For instance, why are you reading this book? To learn how to get positive results in Network Marketing, right? Everything, and I mean *everything* you do, will produce a result.

Here's an example: Let's say you're attempting to ride a bicycle for the first time. Does this imply effort? Sure it does. Now, once you get on the bicycle, are you going to get results? Sure. You may fall down, hit a tree or successfully ride the bicycle. Regardless of the outcome, you will get a result. What if you decide not to get on the bicycle? Will that produce a result? Certainly it will. The result is, you'll never know how to ride a bicycle.

I cannot stress this point enough, so here it is again: EVERYTHING YOU DO WILL ALWAYS PRODUCE A RESULT! The person who gets into a fist fight gets results. The person who refuses to work and goes on welfare also gets results. Even when you sleep at night, your heart is pumping blood throughout your entire body, which in turn keeps you alive. Otherwise, you wouldn't wake up the next morning.

So, in reality, the heart pumping the blood throughout your body is the *effort*, and you staying alive is the *result*.

The definition of *effort* is a voluntary exertion to perform an action; a strenuous attempt. The definition of *result* is a consequence of one's efforts; effect; outcome.

These definitions are further proof that any effort you put into a thing will produce a result. The main reason why you need to realize this is, when people start their own Network Marketing businesses, most of them expect nothing but positive results. When positive results aren't achieved 24 hours a day, 7 days a week, such individuals tend to get nervous.

The reason for this nervousness is the thought of getting no results for all the efforts they put in for that day. This makes them feel worthless. They fail to realize they did get results, but the results were negative ones. But that's okay, at least you're getting results. As long as you realize this, you won't feel totally worthless. Thus, negative results are better than no results at all. However, if you don't turn your negative results into positive ones, you'll eventually go broke.

Now, I'm sure the people who say they're getting no results are speaking of getting no positive results. It's easy to see why they would think that way. But rest assured, you are getting results. Negative results occur when we try to complicate a simplistic business; or when we try to take short cuts; or when we try to re-invent the wheel. The biggest reason, however, for negative results is - doing nothing. That's when you're sure to fail in this business.

If you take your product, and you go out and share it with people, is that putting effort into your business? Of course it is. When they try the products and services, like them and buy them, is that a result? Sure. And it's the good kind of result, a positive one. Now, if you take your product, throw it in your garage and expect it to sell itself, is that an effort? Sure. You had to carry your product all the way to the garage, right?

What results will you achieve by doing this? Most people by now are still saying, "None." That's not true. The results you'll achieve from doing this is that you'll go broke. Is going broke a result? A result of what? Negative efforts. The bottom line is, positive efforts beget positive results, and negative efforts beget negative results.

Obviously, we get paid more for our positive results than we do our negative results. Unfair? Not really. Let's put it into a story:

Let's say you were working real hard building your business, and you were achieving a lot of positive results. With each passing month, your group was growing and so was your income. As a matter of fact, within three years, you were earning more in one month than you did in a year with your ex-job. How would you feel?

To celebrate your success, you and your spouse decided to have a new house built in your favorite part of the country. When you arrived there, you started looking at the pieces of land that were for sale. After only a couple of hours, you both mutually agreed on a certain piece of land.

The next step was to find the best architect in the area and see if he/she could design the house the two of you had been envisioning. The architect drew up your blueprints exactly the way you both wanted it. He/she then referred you to a builder in the area who had a fine reputation. After the meeting with the builder, everything was set. The only thing you needed to do was leave a deposit with the builder. You agreed to pay the remainder of the balance upon completion of the house.

A month later, you flew down again to see if any progress was being made. To your surprise, there were at least 15 men working like crazy putting the foundation of your house together. The foreman recognized you both and came over to tell you that everything was moving ahead of schedule, and your house would be finished a month ahead of the original date you agreed upon.

Excited, you both went to a furniture store and began to look around. Within minutes, you found the perfect patio furniture for the deck you were having built next to the pool. You both agreed to buy it, but you didn't know where to store it until the house was completed. You explained the situation to the manager of the store, and she agreed to hold it for you.

After leaving the furniture store, you decided to hire a landscaper. In no time, a beautiful landscape was designed. After that was settled, you flew back home.

Four months passed, and you finally received the call you'd been waiting for from the builder. He called to tell you that your home was finished, and everything was ready for you to move in. The electricity was on, the gas was on and so was the water. After you hung up with the builder, you called the airlines and booked the first flight you could get.

When you arrived, you took one look at your new home, and everything looked great! The red brick driveway you ordered looked beautiful! The two of you marveled at the landscaping. Every tree was exactly where you wanted it, and every bush was trimmed perfectly. The grounds were immaculate!

When you walked out back, you were in awe. The deck was beautiful and so was the pool. The house looked perfect. Every color and every design was just right!

After seeing the back, you walked back around to the front to enter your new home for the very first time. Would you be excited? I would!

As you opened the front door, you realized it was very bright inside the house. It looked great, but something didn't feel right. You looked around and everything looked fine. Then, after looking up, you realized why it was so bright; the builder forgot to put a roof on your house!

How would you feel now? Would you be disappointed? Would you pay the balance that was due? Why not? Look at all the time, effort and money the builder put into your home. I mean, he put six months into it, while employing 15 men to help him. They worked real hard building your house. You personally witnessed it yourself when you flew down to check the progress they were making. These men deserve to be paid from the builder, don't they? Sure they do! They did what they were supposed to do, but did the builder? No way.

He didn't finish the job he was being paid to do. Therefore, he shouldn't get paid the balance until he finishes the project. Even though he did complete about 90% of your home exactly the way you wanted it, the end result was a negative one. Do you think the builder would learn from this negative result? Sure. He would learn another way not to build a house. Do you think he would finish the job? Yes. Otherwise, he wouldn't get paid the balance. Do you think he would ever do it again? No way. Not if he wanted to stay in business.

The point for this story is, when you set out to do something, remember - everything you do will produce a result. Sometimes the results will not be immediately noticeable. If you cut corners, like the builder, sooner or later it will come back to haunt you. Therefore, to save time, money and your sanity, remember - you will either reap the benefits tomorrow (your goals and dreams) from your actions today, or you will pay the price of failure. *It's up to you.*

So, when you set out to build your business, it's imperative to remember that we learn more from our negative results, but we get paid more for our positive results! And like the builder, you also have the power to turn your negatives into positives. Therefore, learn from your negative results, correct them, and do this business right! I can assure you, doing this business the right way will pay far better dividends to you in the end.

A first-class

effort

will never produce

a second-class

result.

16

What's More Important...
Money or You?

A few years ago, there was this very rich and very miserable man. Every day after lunch, he would leave his office and go the bank to make his daily deposit. He would always push aside anyone who would cross his path. As always, he never said hello to anyone. But this day was to be different. He was about to have his life changed forever.

On his way to the bank he heard a voice say, "Good afternoon, sir, isn't it great to be alive?" The miserable rich man turned around as if to say, "What's so great about it," but saw no one behind him. So he continued on his way. Just then, the same voice shouted, "Have a great day, sir, and may God bless you!" The rich man curiously turned around again. This time, after looking down, he saw the man who was talking to him.

This man was crossing the street using his arms. He had no legs! He lost his legs a few years back because of a machinery accident during which time he saved his co-worker's life. Here's how it happened:

The hydraulic lift on the crane they were operating ceased to function, and 4 cargo boxes fell from the crane. His co-worker was underneath the crane and would have been crushed to death had it not been for him. He dove underneath the crane, and pushed his co-worker out of the way.

His work-mate escaped uninjured. But he wasn't so lucky. The cargo boxes landed on his legs and crushed them instantly. The company honored him as a hero for his bravery, but it cost him his legs to earn such an honor.

Now, back to the story.

Once again, the crippled man shouted out as he continued to cross the street, "Isn't it great to be alive?" He was using 2 padded blocks of wood which were strapped to his hands so that he wouldn't have to use his bare hands to get around. He also wore arm pads on his elbows, just in case he lost his strength and fell to the ground.

After watching this truly blessed man cross the street with no legs, the miserable rich man stopped dead in his tracks and thought to himself, "What am I complaining about? I am a very wealthy and very healthy man, and I'm miserable. This poor man has no legs; yet he possesses the world's greatest commodity - LIFE! He's alive; I'm dead. I go through all the motions of life, but I'm spiritually dead."

He then continued, "I complain about everything that's wrong; he praises everything that's right. I am miserable; he is happy. I am one of the millions of living dead people merely existing on this planet. While he, even with his handicap, is so alive. He, with no material possessions, has a tremendous outlook on life. While I, on the other hand, can have any material possession I want, and I'm miserable."

At that moment, he realized the fact that money couldn't buy him happiness. He started thinking about his 2 healthy legs and how lucky he was to have them. This made him realize how *precious* his life really was.

This experience excited him so much that instead of going to the bank, the man rushed back to his office. His new outlook on life was obvious, as evidenced by the astonished looks on his employees' faces. It was a joyous event. He called them all by their first names and told them how much he appreciated their help. He then shared his experience with them. The story actually brought tears of joy to their eyes.

"From this day on," he exclaimed, "I will appreciate my life and the lives God has sent to me. I will not complain anymore about what's going wrong with my life, I will only praise the good things. I have been so blind and so selfish that I could not see the precious gifts I possess, such as my legs, my precious legs! I never realized how precious my legs were until today. I probably walk 2 to 3 miles each day, and I have never been thankful for that. Talk about selfish and ungrateful."

He then continued, "We Americans feel a loss of freedom if we do not have an automobile to take us from one place to another. We fail to realize we still have our precious legs. Talk about freedom! God blessed me with 2 healthy legs and a healthy family. They're all healthy from head to foot just like me. Isn't it great to be alive," he shouted. *"ISN'T IT GREAT TO BE ALIVE!"*

Five o'clock came and it was time to go home for the evening. He said hello to everyone he saw while walking to his car. Those who knew him looked at him as if he had lost his mind. They weren't used to this usually unfriendly man smiling and saying hello to everyone. "Wow", exclaimed a neighboring business owner, "Miracles really do happen."

On his way home, he appreciated everything he saw. He saw the sun in the late afternoon sky and felt the rays of sunshine on his face and was thankful for his sight and for his sense of feeling. He heard the birds singing and even the honking horns of vehicles and was thankful for his hearing. He then started to think about his wife and kids. His heart pounded like a beating drum. He started smiling again. He had every reason to! He could not wait to see his family.

When he finally arrived home, he ran into his house and grabbed his wife and threw his arms around her. He then called for the kids. With tears of joy in his eyes he said, "I love you all very much, and I'm thankful for all of you." He then explained his life-changing experience with his family and told them he'd never felt better. He said, "I would pay $1,000,000 to feel this way forever!"

The next morning, the newly changed man looked into the mirror and saw himself in a whole new way. "It was real! It wasn't a dream! Thank you, God," he exclaimed.

On his way to the office, he stopped and picked up flowers for all the women in his office. He also had roses delivered to his wife. He then made reservations at his favorite restaurant for 20 people for 1:00 P.M. that same day.

He invited 18 of his top executives and told them he would be a little late and not to start without him. "Where are you going?" asked one of his employees. "I'm going to find my special friend and ask him to join us for lunch today," he answered.

Then without hesitation, he set out to find him. After driving around for an hour, he finally spotted the man who had helped him change his life just 24 hours ago.

With a burst of energy, he parked his car and ran over to the legless man. His new friend was unaware of what had taken place in the past 24 hours. "Excuse me," the wealthy man said. "Do you remember who I am? I'm the man you spoke to yesterday." "Why no," he said. "I can't say that I do." "Wow!" the rich man thought. "Sharing kindness with the world is second nature to this man. I'll bet his kind words have helped hundreds of people in the past without him even knowing it."

After explaining the situation and the incredible effect it had on his life, his new friend was overjoyed and gladly accepted his invitation to lunch. The rich man offered to carry the legless man to the car, but the legless man refused. "I don't feel sorry for myself. You shouldn't either!"

At the restaurant, he was personally introduced to everyone. He was then seated at the head of the table. After lunch, the newly changed man began to reiterate the past day's events. He then said, "You know, I told my wife yesterday that I would pay $1,000,000 to feel this way forever. Now I'm convinced that I will, and I owe it all to you."

He then presented the man with a check for $1,000,000 (for the way he helped him change his life). The man stared at the check for a moment and then said, "I cannot accept this check. I didn't earn it. For me, it took the loss of my legs to realize how precious my life was. I may have lost 2 legs, but I really ended up gaining, because I learned to appreciate everything I still had. My tragedy turned out to be a pure blessing."

He became teary eyed as he continued, "I have so much to be thankful for, and so do you.

Your new outlook on life didn't come from me, it came from God. He deserves all the credit; not me. Therefore, I cannot accept this check, although I do appreciate the offer."

"You do not have to pay $1,000,000 to feel this way. It's a free gift from God. Once you receive it," he continued, "it's your duty to share this gift with others and hope they will experience the same renewed appreciation for life we're all feeling here today. Once again, I appreciate your very nice offer, but you already gave me the only gift I need from you, your friendship."

* This Story Goes Hand in Hand with the Last Story *

Let's say you were dead broke and you were looking through the Help Wanted section of the newspaper. An advertisement read, "Willing to pay $1,000,000 if you can provide me with what I need." Would you respond? Sure you would!

Now, one hour later, your phone rings. It's the man who put the ad in the paper. Are you excited? He appears to be a very nice man. He begins to tell you how he became a millionaire at the age of 40 and how his company is now a Fortune 500 company.

How do you feel now? Most of us would feel under-qualified because of the negative programming we endured in the past. However,

116

that insecure feeling goes away instantly as he continues, "I'm not looking for a sales person or a manager." "Then what are you looking for?" you ask. "What I am looking for," he replies, "takes no special skill, and it doesn't matter what you've done in the past." Confused, you reply, "I don't understand what it is you want."

"Well, a few years ago," he says, "I finally started to take some time out of my busy schedule to enjoy my success with my family. We built a beautiful vacation home on the beach. We would usually go there 3 or 4 times a year. The sunsets were so beautiful you would think you were in heaven. Imagine that," he continues, "looking out at the ocean with the sun setting so beautifully against the horizon while sitting on your own front porch. You cannot put a price tag on such beauty." "That sounds great," you interrupt, "but what does that have to do with me?"

Suddenly, his voice softens, "A year ago," he says, "I lost my vision due to an unsuccessful eye operation. The only chance I have at ever seeing those beautiful sunsets again would be if someone donates their eyes to me. I have been looking for an eye donor all year with no success. That's why I put the ad in the paper. Now you know what I am in need of. So I ask you, will you sell your eyes to me for $1,000,000?"

"Now, before you give me an answer," he adds, "I will give you 3 days to think about your decision. If in 3 days you are willing, I will pay you $250,000 up front, and the balance after the operation. So don't answer now. I will call you back in 3 days."

After hanging up, you immediately start thinking about his proposal. Gee, do I really need my eyesight? Can I function without it? The money would sure help. It would totally eliminate the financial burden that has been holding me and my family down for years. We could finally take the kids to Disney World and buy that dream car we always wanted.

Then, with a sharp pain in your heart, you'd probably realize the fact that you wouldn't see the smiles on your kids faces when they saw Mickey Mouse, and you would never be able to drive your dream car because of your new disability. What would you do? Would you keep your eyesight? Or would you trade it for the $1,000,000?

If you answered, "Yes, I would trade my eyesight for $1,000,000," you really don't understand what life is all about. On the other hand, if you answered, "No, there is no way I would trade my vision for $1,000,000 or any amount for that matter," you are one BIG step closer to true wealth.

Once you realize the saying, *"It's not what you have or what you do, it's what you do with what you have!"* you are even one step closer.

There is nothing in this world that you want so desperately, that God didn't give you the talent to get. I have to emphasize the words *"want so desperately"* because a lot of people want certain things in their lives, but are unwilling to do what it takes to get them. Face it, everything you have in life right now is there because you were willing to do whatever it took to get them. So, if you want to have the finest things life has to offer, you MUST be willing to do what it takes to get them also.

To get ahead in life, you do not have to sell your gifts from God (e.g. selling your eyes for $1,000,000). In reality, that would only set you back further. Once you stop worrying about what you DON'T have, and focus on what you DO have and you use it to its fullest, you won't be stopped from fulfilling your true purpose in life.

Now, some of you may be asking yourselves, "These stories are great, but what do they have to do with my success?" The answer to this question is "EVERYTHING!"

The sole purpose for these stories is to help you realize the fact that you really do possess everything you need to become successful. **You always have!** All you lacked in the past was the realization of this fact. Now that you know this, let's put your awesome God-given talents together with our awesome training, and let's get busy building your future! *Success is not difficult, but people are.* DO NOT complicate this training! It was meant to be simplistic. It's not broke, so don't try to fix it.

Now for some more good news: Did you know that it's easier to become wealthy in America than it is to work for a living? Sure, that's because there's much less competition. Over 95% of Americans are willing to work for someone else, while the rest of us (5%) work for ourselves. Working for yourself is definitely the least traveled road, but it's the most successful road! That's why it's easier (not simpler), to become wealthy.

Everyone in America wants success! Most of us, however, are unwilling to take the less traveled road.

YOU DID!

You see, this is even further proof (if you need more proof) that you are unique. You did make the right choice! You are one of the top 5% group! You do work for yourself! Even if it's only part time for now, that's okay. At least you're on the right track! So keep moving and never quit! Most importantly, never forget:

I __(NAME)__, am already a very wealthy person, and I have all the tools I need to take my business to the top. I know success is coming to me. I can feel it. I can see it. The very best that life has to offer me will be mine. Why?

Because I'm worth it. I just have to earn it. I truly believe in myself, and I am willing to do whatever I have to for my future.

Remember: You can go anywhere in the world looking for someone exactly like yourself, and after years of searching, I can guarantee you, no one will even come close to being exactly like you. Remember, I'm an identical twin. We have a lot in common, but we also have many differences. Face it, we are all unique. This includes YOU too! There never has been or never will be another you. You are one in a billion. With odds like that, how can you lose?

Therefore, if you do not act now and go for your dreams, you WILL regret it later. That's a promise from me to you. Do not settle for mediocrity! You deserve so much more than that. That is, if you think you do. Do you?

Success

is simply a matter of

luck,

ask any failure.

Part Three

Caring

is

Sharing

The one thing

worse than a quitter

is the man who is afraid

to begin.

17

The Upper Echelon

Did you know that retailing your products and services can and should be a lot of fun? It really can be! That is, once you learn how to successfully do it. This section of the book is designed to do just that - teach you how. I'm sure you're aware of the fact that the word *"sell"* scares most of us to death. If it scares you too, after reading this section, you'll have a totally different view on sales. When you finish, you'll realize there is nothing at all to be afraid of.

Most of us perceive sales to be a lot of high pressuring and forcing others into buying things they really don't want or need. And for a lot of sales people, this is a proper perception. However, the ones who make the most money in sales do not high pressure anyone! Nor do they force feed their products and services down their potential customers' throats.

Did you know there is a 20-80 rule in sales? *Sure!* 20% of us who are involved in sales actually make 80% of the sales, and the majority of us (80%) sell only 20%. On top of that, 20% of us sell 80% of our customers, while 80% of us sell only 20%. Most importantly, however, 20% of us make 80% of the money while the majority of us (80%) make only 20% of it.

Question: How do people become 20%'ers? Do they get there from going to college? Not necessarily. It's amazing how many of us spend 4 years of our lives and a lot of money going to college to learn marketing, thinking we'll have it made after we graduate. This thought motivates us to work hard and get good grades. However, after graduation, most of us start to realize we learned little or nothing about sales.

Now, this book was not written to knock going to college. I'm all for college. It can be quite an experience. It offers advanced education for all who attend. For some people, it can really open up doors in the future. But once again, for the majority, although they learn a lot, this knowledge has little or nothing to do with the real world. *Fact is, the ones who strive for and eventually make it BIG in sales (the 20% group), for the most part, get there by listening to and duplicating the people who have already been there and done it.*

It's next to impossible to learn how to become the best in any profession from someone who has never done it before. I mean, if you wanted to become a doctor, would you go to a lawyer to be trained? Of course not. You would go to a doctor, right? Yes, I know you have to go to college first. But until you actually go into the operating room and watch and learn from the best, it will be next to impossible for you to become one of the best yourself.

The same thing goes with becoming an attorney. Do you think education alone will make a person a top lawyer? No way. Again, education is important. However, the ones who want to become the best are constantly in court rooms (during their free time) watching the experienced professionals do their thing. Do you think aspiring attorneys around the country were watching the O.J. Simpson trial? Sure they were! That's because they wanted to study and learn from the very best. And with television, it was possible for them to watch and learn without even leaving their homes.

Now, there are some self-made 20%'ers. These people are naturals. They go out and make a fortune by learning on their own. The majority of us, however, need to be trained. The bottom line is - if you want to be the best in your field, you need to learn from the best in your field. It's that simple! Yes, education is vitally important, but it's NOT the only thing needed.

Here's another example: If you wanted to put an in-ground swimming pool in your back yard, and I educated you on how to do it (by means of lectures, books and video tapes), would you be able to immediately go out and do the job? Probably not. Until you watch me or someone else actually install a pool (O.J.T.), it will be very difficult for you to do it yourself.

My point again is education is very important. But in my opinion, the "on the job training" is even more important. Therefore, it's of extreme urgency for you to learn from the best in your field. The good news is this industry is full of 20%'ers. Further, unlike most industries, they are both ready and willing to train you.

Now, out of the two groups (the 20%'ers and the 80%'ers), which one do you want to be in? I'm sure you want to be in the 20% group, right? Everyone wants to be in the 20% group. Few of us, however, are willing to do what it takes to get there, just like all the other high-prestige groups.

This is sad, because the people in the 20% group DO NOT do things much differently than the majority of us do. In fact, they don't work any harder. They just work smarter! It's true. They do a few things differently than the rest of us. The things they do differently, however, is what elevates them above everyone else.

Let's talk about some of the things the 20%'ers do differently than the 80%'ers:

First of all, it starts with a personal commitment. This elite group realizes that, in order to get there, one MUST be totally committed to getting there. Once this commitment is made, if serious, that person will be more than half way there without even doing a thing. In other words, the proper foundation for success will begin to be laid on a single commitment. That's how important and powerful this commitment really is!

The next thing 20%'ers realize is, when dealing with a client or prospect, they are not dealing with a sucker or a victim. They, like you, are dealing with *people!* They treat EVERYONE they are dealing with as if it was their mother. Imagine that, treating everyone you come in contact with as if it was your mother.

From start to finish, 20%'ers are constantly treating their customers (friends) like gold. They do not falsely flatter them the way most smooth-talking slicksters do. In fact, it's quite the opposite. They actually APPRECIATE the fact that they even have a customer in the first place who they can SHARE their products and services with. They know the potential customer wants to be in control and wants to feel appreciated. And if he/she is, the chances of making a sale is much higher. The bottom line is: No sale - No money.

Another thing 20%'ers do is THEY LISTEN to their customers. Let's face it, you cannot tell your customer what he/she wants to purchase, they have to tell you! The only way they can tell you is if you listen to them. Which brings us to a good point. 20%'ers talk (to their customers) 20% of the time and listen 80% of the time. The 80%'ers, on the other hand, talk 80% of the time and listen only 20% of the time. 20%'ers listen so much because they truly **care** about what their customers want.

That's just it! If I had to sum up in two words the main thing 20%'ers do differently than the 80%'ers is - *THEY CARE!* They truly care about EVERY person they come in contact with. And when you truly care for your customers, you will go out of your way and do whatever it takes to make sure they are comfortable. What does the customer want to feel comfortable about? That's an easy one. They want to feel comfortable with the product, the price, the warranty (if available), and most importantly - YOU!

I'm sure it's becoming quite obvious to you as to **"why"** the 20%'ers make more sales, friends and money than the 80%'ers. Again, they work SMARTER and FRIENDLIER, not HARDER and MEANER. And you thought the ones at the top in sales were sharks, huh? Now you know it's the exact opposite.

I know it almost sounds too good to be true. However, the fact that they **care** about their customers and **appreciate** them really does put them head and shoulders above the rest. Add that to their personal commitment (to want to be a 20%'er), and I'd say that's a pretty good foundation. Wouldn't you? A foundation, however, is just the beginning. So without further ado, let's teach you the rest of what it takes to be a 20%'er. Fair enough?

The upcoming chapters are chock full of information which will further help you reach the top 20% echelon. Try it on for size. If it fits, wear it. If not, you can always take it off and continue to do what you were previously doing. It's your business. Therefore, it's your choice.

One more thing: We all know the odds of becoming a professional athlete, a movie star or a multi-millionaire are quite slim. In fact, they are so slim, most of us wouldn't even consider them as a career. The odds are virtually one in a million. And with odds like that, most of us feel we don't even have a chance.

There are many, many professions where the odds of just getting there are extremely low. A head coach in the NFL, for instance, is a very tough job to get. I mean, think about it, how many people around the world love the NFL? Further, how many people would love to coach in the NFL? Most of us, right? Now, for the sobering facts: Out of all the millions of us who would love to coach in the NFL, there are only 30 NFL teams, and all of them already have head coaches! Talk about slim.

Let's take another profession: How about a U.S. Governor? Out of all the millions of people who would love to become a U.S. Governor, only 50 people can be elected every four years. How about the President? There are roughly 250,000,000 people living in America. How many Americans would love to become President? How many of us can become the President? One. Forget that profession.

Now for the good news: What group are you looking to get into? The 20% group, right? Well, after discussing the odds of those other professions, 20% should be a breath of fresh air to you. I mean, think about it, 2 out of every 10 people in sales form this successful group (upper echelon). Or, in simpler terms, 1 out of every 5. Pretty attainable, huh? I'll take those odds over one in a million any day. How about you?

Flying first class

is not an acquired taste.

One takes to it

immediately.

18

Retailing Your Products and Services

How many people do you know who like to be sold? No one, right? On the other hand, how many people do you know who like to buy? *Everyone does!* It's true. Fact is - *Everyone likes to buy. No one, however, likes to be sold.* Since this is the case, why are so many salespeople trained to hard sell and close the customer, when that's not what the customer wants? Could this be the reason why the national closing rate is only around 20%? Sure it is. Here's why:

When we try to hard sell our potential customers into buying, what we also do is take control away from them. This makes them nervous. When they're nervous, it's almost impossible for them to relax. And if they're not relaxed, they won't feel like buying, no matter what kind of deal we may be offering.

Therefore, the name of the game for success in sales is not to hard close and pressure the customer. What is, however, is to make the customer feel comfortable. How can our potential customers feel comfortable if we try to shove our products and services down their throats? The answer is - they can't. Would you feel comfortable if they did it to you? Probably not, right? Well then, why should we do it to them?

Some companies today are finally starting to realize the fact that high pressuring the customer is NOT the most effective way to market their products and services and have stopped using that approach. Most companies, however, still do. For instance, a lot of franchise clothing stores today are too pushy! As soon as you walk into their store, they're all over you. It's like you can almost hear the sound of *"wasps"* attacking you. How can anyone feel comfortable in that situation? I know I sure don't.

On the other hand, do you think these companies would sell more clothing if they tried the no-pressure approach instead of the one they normally use? Let's take a look and see:

Let's say you were looking to buy some new outfits. As you entered the store, you expected to be harassed as usual. This time, however, to your surprise, it was much different. The manager of the store came up to you and said, "I just want you to know we have changed our ways. We no longer use the high-pressure approach. In other words, I'm not going to bother you one bit. The store is all yours. Look as long as you'd like and try on whatever you want. If, and only if you need me, I'll be over there. I really hope you find what you're looking for."

Now, let's be honest, if the manager of the store used this approach on you (instead of the normal high-pressure approach), how would you feel? Would you buy something? Sure you would! How could you not want to buy something?! I mean, the manager just gave you COMPLETE control of the store. I would feel almost obligated to buy something just because of how good the manager made me feel.

Now, since this approach would bring more sales to the store, how come more companies don't use it? This really blows my mind! Fact is, most companies today are too paranoid! They feel that if they don't corner the customer and pressure them into buying, the customer will leave the store without purchasing anything at all.

Actually, the exact opposite is the truth. If the manager of the store does corner his/her customers, that's when they'll feel uncomfortable and want to leave. The bottom line is, the more comfortable the customer feels, the longer he/she will stay. And the longer he/she stays, the better the chances are that they will purchase something. This is just common sense. Wouldn't you agree?

The same thing goes with us. The more we try to shove our products and services down our potential customers' throats, the harder it will be for us to sell them. Therefore, the *KEY* to successfully retailing in Network Marketing or in any industry, for that matter, is not to *SELL* what we have, but *SHARE* it.

What do I mean when I say share? That's simple. Did you ever purchase a product that you liked so much, you shared it with a friend, who after using it, purchased it also? That's all sharing is - finding a product, buying it, using it, liking it, and then sharing it with others.

I mean think about it, if you go to a restaurant, and the food is good, are you going to tell your friends about it? I would certainly hope so. That's what sharing is all about. Now, when your friends go to the restaurant, are you going to get a commission check from the owner of the restaurant for telling your friends to eat there? *No!* Why not? You won't even get a discount when you go back there to eat again, will you?

Let's face it, we have been sharing products and services with our families and friends our whole lives. Further, we've been doing it without being compensated or even thanked from the manufacturers, retail outlets, restaurants, etc., who have prospered from us doing it.

In Network Marketing, we do the same thing. We get turned on to a super product or service, we use them, we love them, and then we **SHARE** *(not sell)* them with the people we know. The only difference, however, is we get paid to do it. *What a concept!*

Now some of you may say, "I could never make money off my friends!" If this is you, let's put it into a story:

Let's say you were a realtor. One day, you received a phone call from one of your friends. He/she was looking to buy a new home. Would you help him/her? I would certainly hope so. I mean, if you were my friend, I sure hope you would help me. Just like you would expect me to help you, right? Okay, we both agree the right thing to do would be to help your friend. So out you would go to find your friend a new home.

Now, let's say that after putting a lot of time into the deal, you finally found the perfect home for your friend. When it came time to close the deal, would you say to him/her, "You know, I just realized, we're friends. I can't sell you this house. If I do, I'll make a commission. That just wouldn't be right." Or, would you sell him/her the house?

Truth is, if you don't sell him/her the house, someone else will. Besides, don't you feel your friends will trust you more than they would a stranger? Sure they will! Therefore, when YOU share your products and services with them, they will feel more comfortable about their purchase. That's because they already trust you. Makes sense, doesn't it?

I know that if there was a product or service I was interested in, and a friend of mine either sold it or knew how to get it, I would definitely get it through him/her. Your friends will too! Therefore, you should feel it's your duty to share what you have with everyone you know.

Knowing this, it just wouldn't make sense for you to get involved in Network Marketing, love the products and services, share them with your family and friends, have them love them, and then not sell to them because you'd feel it wouldn't be right to earn a commission. Sounds pretty ridiculous, huh? If this is the approach you're planning on taking, you will not be very successful in this industry.

Besides, by sharing with your family and friends, you're also helping them. Why? Because every product and service I have personally seen in this industry is truly state of the art. These products and services are phenomenal! Whenever there is a nucleus like that, demand always follows. Therefore, your family and friends will eventually have them whether you sell them to them or not.

The fact that this industry offers phenomenal products and services is great. However, we need to constantly remember that *no one likes to be sold!* Not even mom and dad. But everyone likes to buy! So if you want to sell to only 20% of your family and friends (by using the high-pressure approach), that's up to you. On the other hand, if you want to sell to most of them (approximately 80%), you need to **SHARE** what you have with them and let them decide for themselves. The results you'll achieve by **SHARING** *(not selling)* will amaze you.

Now, before you can even think of retailing your products and services to anyone else, there is one crucial thing you must do. YOU MUST BE SOLD ON THEM FIRST! That's what the next chapter is all about.

Even if you're on the

right track,

you'll get run over if you

just sit there.

19

The Best Satisfied Customer is Yourself

Distribution of the products and services you represent is definitely the *backbone* of Network Marketing. As a matter of fact, it's the backbone of any industry! You can have the greatest people in your company and the greatest products and services, but if they're not being sold, how will your company survive? The answer is - it can't! Hence, distribution is the *bloodline* of your company's survival.

Knowing this, if you're new in this industry or part time, your job is simple - CONSTANTLY RETAIL AND DISTRIBUTE YOUR PRODUCTS AND SERVICES (More on distribution later). This will keep your bloodline flowing smoothly. This is especially true in Network Marketing.

Here's why: Everyone you share your products and services with, if treated properly, will be your customers for life.

The reason for this is the products and services you represent are not sold in stores. Therefore, they cannot be purchased anywhere except through your company. So, if your customers like you and your products and services, when it comes time to re-order or renew them, it will be an automatic sale for you. It's like money in the bank. This is known as residual income. *Not too shabby, huh?*

Now, in order to successfully share your products and services with others, you need to be a satisfied customer first. There is only one way for you to become a satisfied customer, YOU HAVE TO USE THE PRODUCTS AND SERVICES! I mean, how can you really get excited about a product or a service, without actually using it yourself? You can't!

However, once you do use the products and services you represent, and you personally benefit from using them, your customers will feel your enthusiasm. They will hear it in your voice and see it in your eyes. Believe me, your belief and excitement towards them will be obvious to your potential customers. They'll want to use them just to feel the way you're feeling. But in order for this to happen, you must use them first.

That's why automobile companies give their sales people company "demonstration" vehicles. It's so they can get to know what they're selling. If they sell Ford automobiles, the company doesn't give them a Honda. That just wouldn't make much sense! Therefore, if they're selling Fords, they should be driving Fords. By driving the cars, they'll get to learn firsthand all the vehicle's key features and how to operate them. Then, when the customer asks a question, they'll be prepared. This, in turn, will increase sales.

There are some car sales people who try to get excited about the vehicles without actually driving them. However, in time, it becomes very obvious that their excitement is not genuine. How could it be? Sure, they can read up on the vehicles and learn some of the features, but until they actually drive them, they'll never really know them like they should.

The same thing goes for you! **This is your business!** Therefore, you **M U S T** know your products and services! The best way to do this is to simply use them. Sure you want to read up on them. But until you use them and benefit from them, it will be hard for you to totally believe in them.

Now let's talk about distribution. As you know, this is your business. Therefore, you have to treat it that way. This means you have to be prepared. One key thing you need in order to operate on any given day is inventory. Without it, you're out of business.

It's like if you owned a hot dog stand, and you had no hot dogs to sell, how would you do? Picture this, having someone walk up to you and saying, "Give me a hot dog with everything on it!" What would you do? Would you say, "Gee, I'm sorry. I don't have any hot dogs. I just wanted to see if this idea would work"? Or, would you show that person a picture of a hot dog with everything on it in hopes of satisfying his/her appetite? However creative you would get, the bottom line is, if you have no hot dogs, you'll go broke. **YOU NEED INVENTORY!**

Some people like to order their inventory one piece at a time. I don't recommend (if at all possible) you do this. First of all, if you do do this, every time you make a sale, as you know, you'll make a profit. That's good, but now you're out of business until you re-order. And that could take some time if the product has to be shipped to you.

Second, every time you make a sale, how does it make you feel? It makes you feel great, right? One thing for sure, it's a real momentum builder. However, if you order your inventory one piece at a time, don't you think the wait will hurt your momentum? Sure it will! Every time you have positive momentum building, believe me, you want nothing to stop it. Not having extra inventory on hand is definitely a sure-fire way to not only slow your momentum, but kill it. In my opinion, it's not worth the risk.

140

Third, if you're looking to become successful, you should always be talking about your business. If you are, there's no telling when or where your next sale will take place. Therefore, like the hot dog stand scenario, if you're unprepared for business, you're out of business!

Fourth, you're looking to build a large group of distributors, right? Well then, don't you think you owe it to them (especially your new distributors) to have extra inventory on hand so they can get off to a fast start? You wouldn't want to slow their momentum, would you?

Fifth, by ordering extra inventory, it will just flat out reconfirm your commitment about wanting to become successful in this industry. And, believe me, it will definitely show. Not to mention your new people; they will not listen to what you say, but they will do what you do. In other words, if you order your inventory one piece at a time, there's a good chance you'll find them doing the exact same thing. However, if you order in bulk, there's a good chance that they will too!

Having extra inventory on hand (product, training materials, etc.) is just plain smart. Besides being smart, it shows you really care. When your new distributors get involved, in my opinion, it's imperative to have product on hand for them. This doesn't mean you should give it to them. No. Pass it on to them at the wholesale price they're entitled to. Then, simply re-order from the company. It's a great concept. You get to help your new distributors (and believe me, they'll appreciate you for it) and make money at the same time.

So you see, your commitment to having extra inventory is not only important to you. What you do will be seen and probably duplicated by the people in your group. This doesn't mean that if you don't have the money, you should go out and rob a bank to get the money for extra inventory. If you can't do it, don't do it. However, if you can do it, I think I just gave you **5 great reasons** to do so. However, before you even think of distributing products and services to the people in your group, I highly recommend you become your best customer. Wouldn't you agree?

Everyone believes.

Some believe their

beliefs,

others believe their

doubts.

20

Try it You'll Like it

How many of us like to try things for free? That's easy. Most of us. How many of us like to give our opinions on things? Again, most of us. That's why the *"try it you'll like it"* and *"free sample"* approaches work as well as they do. It's because everyone gets to try the products and services and give their opinions on them first, before actually buying them.

If you want your sales to absolutely skyrocket, I highly recommend you use these approaches (if possible). Think about it, all you have to do is get really excited about your products and services and then share them with the people you know. Once they try them, and the products and services work the way you say they will, and they like them, they'll buy them. *It's that simple!* Again, it's all based on the premise that you want their opinion.

Now, when you're ready to share your products and services with others, and you want to use this approach, you can do it one of two ways. You can either call them on the phone or you can stop by their homes.

If you decide to call them, when you get them on the line, NEVER rush right into your reason for calling. Instead, talk about the things you would normally talk about. Then, after awhile, say something like this, "By the way, before I forget, the reason I'm calling you is to let you know that I'm starting (or thinking about starting) a part-time business. Obviously I'm very excited. But before I totally commit to starting, I would really like to get your opinion on the products and services I'll be marketing. Your opinion really means a lot to me. Would you mind helping me out?"

Most people, after being complimented like that, will be more than happy to help you.

Now, if you're planning on stopping by their homes (instead of calling), use the same approach. In other words, don't rush right into your reason for being there. Just be yourself! Remember, these people were your family and friends long before you got involved in this industry. Therefore, if you go into their homes acting any differently than you normally would, it will be very obvious to them.

One more thing: If you normally go to their homes wearing a suit, it will look normal if you do so now. But if you never wore a suit when you went to their homes in the past, don't wear one now. Think about it, these people will think you're a salesman. You won't even have a chance! They won't even listen to you! Therefore, go to their homes dressed the way you would normally dress.

Once again, however, you need to remember that this is a non-threatening approach! You are not going to their homes to sell them anything, you're going to get their advice! Therefore, DO NOT TRY TO SHOVE YOUR PRODUCTS, SERVICES OR OPPORTUNITY DOWN THEIR THROATS! This is the *"try it you'll like approach,"* not the *"shove it down their throats and get thrown out of their house as fast as I can approach!"*

In other words, after you give your products and services to them, (if you don't have other plans together) you should simply leave. If you decide you're going to hang out and badger them to buy, they'll probably end up throwing you and what you're offering out the door, no matter how good of friends you may be! I do not recommend you do this. **Do it the right way.** It pays better.

Knowing this, if you're the type of person who gets real nervous when it comes time to sharing your products and services, **no more excuses!** You now have a non-threatening approach that is not only simple to use, but anyone can do it - including you. *What a concept!*

Once again, however, you must be **EXCITED** about what you have! Then and only then should you share it. The good news is most people will be more than happy to give you their opinions. That is, if you give them a reason to (i.e., your total faith and belief in what you represent).

With these 2 approaches, the only way your potential customers can give you their opinions will be for them to try your products and services for a couple of days. This is great news because the more exposure they have to them, the more accustomed they'll get. When this happens and they like them, you'll have another customer.

Did you notice I've said nothing about money yet? That's because the money part of the deal shouldn't even be mentioned unless they mention it. Remember, you're asking them for their opinions, not their money!

This doesn't mean you should avoid talking about the prices of your products and services. YOU SHOULD BE PROUD OF THEM! Just don't focus on the cash transaction. Face it, them buying your products and services is the last step of the deal. Therefore, let it be the last thing you focus on. In other words, don't become greedy and speed up the process by trying to close the sale before you should. This is a very effective approach! Let it take its natural course.

In my opinion, when done right, the *"try it you'll like it"* and the *"free sample"* approaches are the most incredible and lucrative approaches we can use. I mean think about it, the closing rate with these two approaches is around 70%-80% and higher (as compared to the 20% closing percentage with the high-pressure approach). That's because there is no pressure on the potential customer. In other words, he/she is in COMPLETE control. That's the way it should be.

Many established industries today are now realizing this and using this approach. For instance, some leading automobile companies are now letting their customers drive a brand new vehicle for one month free! At month's end, if they're not 100% satisfied with the car, all they have to do is return it to the dealership at no obligation to them whatsoever. Of course, if they like the car, they can purchase it at the price they both agree upon.

Automobile dealers would NEVER take such a high risk if they thought it wouldn't be a successful one. Think about it, you do not just let $20,000 vehicles leave your dealership for one month, unless you are very confident the potential customer will purchase it. That's just it! After driving their dream car for one month, if they can afford it, why would they not want to purchase it? Would you? You see, it does make sense.

Home builders are also using this approach! They now decorate some of their homes and call them their "model homes" so the potential customer can see what the house will look like when it's finished. Now, some of you may say, "They've been doing this for years!" You're right. They have been

147

doing this for years. But now it's being done without sales people. Now, the potential customers come and go at their free will (without a sales person one step behind) and only commit to purchasing when they are ready.

Here's another example: Cable television. Cable companies are sending representatives out to our homes and also advertising on television to ask us if we would like to try their services for one month absolutely free. Our only obligation is to try it for the month, and then, if we like it, we can keep it.

The funny thing is, at month's end, over 80% of us who try it and use it for the month end up keeping it. The majority of us figure $5 - $40 per month is a good price to pay to have good entertainment and better reception. Not to mention the kids. Face it, once they watch the Disney channel, it's all over! You wouldn't be able to get rid of it even if you tried.

I'm convinced beyond a shadow of a doubt that if more companies used this approach, their sales would skyrocket!

Here is yet another example: Let's say I owned a pet store. You came in one day, and you saw this puppy dog, and you instantly fell in love with it.

After noticing you, I walked over to you and said, "Isn't she a beautiful puppy?" You then said, "She sure is! I would love to take her home with me, but I don't have the money." I then said, "That's okay, why don't you take the puppy home with you for a couple of days for *free* to see if you're compatible with one another? If you are, great! If not, bring her back. There will be no obligation to you."

What would you do? Would you take the puppy home? If so, do you really think you'd return the puppy after one week? Be honest. The truth is very few of us would. I know I wouldn't. In fact, 80% - 95% of us would keep the puppy.

The funny thing is the puppy would do her thing all over your carpet, chew all the wires in your house and rip holes in your furniture. In other words, the dog would drive you absolutely NUTS! Yet, you'll do anything and everything in your power to keep her. Why? Because she would grow on you. That's why. Case closed!

This happens with any product or service. After awhile, they just flat out grow on us. Whatever the reasons - convenience, price, quality, beauty, features, etc. - they just grow on us.

Even things we can't keep have this effect on us. For instance, have you ever gone on vacation where you stayed in a hotel for a week or two? What happened? If you're like me, the room grew on you, right? Fact is, it grows on us so much that we don't want to leave. We actually feel like we're leaving something behind. One thing for sure is, next time we stay there, we'll probably request to stay in that same room.

The same thing goes with a rental car. We actually think it's our car after awhile. Sure we beat them! But you have to admit, the car does grow on you.

After a product or service becomes part of our daily lives, it's very hard to give them back. Knowing this, my advice is, if there is any way for you to let your potential customers try your products and services first, before purchasing them, DO IT! Your sales will skyrocket just like all the other companies who are now prospering from it. If they do it, why shouldn't you?

The *"try it you'll like it"* and the *"free sample"* approaches are definitely the best ways for you to make more sales without actually selling. As we already mentioned, it will increase your closing percentage from around 20% all the way up to 80% and higher! If you've never tried these two approaches, you really don't know what you're missing.

Besides, when you use these two awesome approaches, you will not be high pressuring or hard closing anyone! On the contrary, you'll be making a lot of customers, a lot of money, and a lot of friends. Now, that's what I call success.

The man who wakes up

and finds himself

successful

hasn't been asleep.

21

Learn from Television

Did you ever watch a television commercial? Did you really watch it? It's amazing how companies utilize anywhere from 30 seconds to a minute of air time to sell us their products and services. If you think about it, a television commercial is simply a short story. That's it. In this short story, they'll show a problem. Then, they'll show their products and services fixing the problem. Then, of course, they'll show the satisfied customer in the end.

The problems they'll show being fixed, however, are usually extremely fabricated. That's because the commercial is made with what we WANT in mind, not with what we NEED. Confused? Let's give you an example:

Let's say a company is shooting a commercial to sell us bubble gum. Do you think they know upfront our kids don't need bubble gum? *Sure they do!* They know it's not good for us. Therefore, why mention it! That just wouldn't make good business sense. Instead, they'll create a WANT. They may say that if our kids purchase their bubble gum, they'll be able to blow the biggest bubbles on the planet, which in turn will make them super cool.

If they're selling perfume or cologne, they know we don't need chemical-filled products on our skin either! That's why they'll create the illusion that if we use their perfume or cologne, we will all of a sudden be sought after by every babe in town. This is what we want, right? Sure it is! At least that's what most of us want.

Fact is, we probably don't need many of the products and services that are sold on television. But we do WANT to be *cool,* and we do WANT to be *sought after.* And believe me, they (the companies) realize this fact.

Therefore, if they want to successfully market their products and services to us, they can't focus on what we don't need, they MUST focus on what we WANT. And the companies who create a serious WANT are the ones who control their industries. It's that simple!

Television commercials are never too factual. Why? Because most people don't want to hear too many facts. We want to hear stories! Companies realize this. That's why they rarely mention the technical features of their products and services. They know that too many facts will bore most people. But stories always keep our attention.

Another thing these companies rarely focus on is the price of their products and services. Think about it, the companies who run commercials on television offer premium products and services. They're aware of the fact that there are similar products and services on the market for less money. Knowing this, they don't focus on the price, again, they focus on creating a *want.* Their job is to create a WANT so big, that the price will be no object to the viewer.

Here is an example of an ordinary television commercial: Since we're in the computer age, let's create a computer commercial. Let's say the commercial starts off with a split screen. On one side, we'll see a man who is obviously stressed out. He has a desk full of unfinished paperwork. He is definitely not a happy camper.

On the other side, we'll see a man conveniently using their computer and having a blast in doing so. Obviously, he has no unfinished paperwork on his desk. He couldn't be happier!

The commercial will then show the computer up close. This is where they'll show us and sell us on a few of its features. And then, of course, they'll mention the simplicity of how to use the computer, the time it will save us over not having one, how much better their computer is (as compared to the competition), and then, of course, how affordable it will be for us if we act right now.

After that, they'll go back to the split screen. The clocks on the walls behind the desks will show 8:00 P.M. What do you think the man who was so overwhelmed with paperwork is doing at this hour? You got it. He's still at his desk working. What about the man who owns their computer? What is he doing? He's either out playing tennis with his partner or walking the beach with his wife.

Question: What does playing tennis or walking the beach have to do with buying a computer? Nothing, right? I'm sure this man played tennis and walked the beach with his wife long before he purchased their computer. The reason why the company shows us this, however, is because they know this is what we WANT more of in life. Therefore, we're not really sold on the computer, we're sold on the freedom and the relaxation the computer will add to our lives.

This is just further proof that if you want to make a lot of money, sell people what they want. Everyone of us WANTS to have more fun, look better, smell better, spend more time at home with our families, be the talk of the town, etc. The companies who successfully sell us these things will make the most money. *It's that simple!*

Beer companies have been doing this for years. They don't sell us on the beer. Fact is, WE DON'T NEED BEER! So instead of selling us beer, they'll sell us the illusion that if we buy their beer, we'll be drinking it with the "Swedish bikini team". Then, a crate of lobsters will parachute out of the sky just for us. Cooked! Or, we'll see 4 men sitting around a campfire proclaiming, *"It just doesn't get any better than this!"*

Now, I do agree that sitting around a campfire with good friends is a great time. And I'm sure partying with the "Swedish bikini team" and eating fresh flown-in lobster would be great too! But what does beer have to do with it? I can honestly tell you that I never once had the "Swedish bikini team" come knocking on my door after purchasing a case of their beer. *Did you?*

The funniest thing about these commercials is everyone looks and is built so great! Maybe it's me, but everyone I know who drinks a lot of beer does not look like the people in the commercials. If they did, I would think beer was a miracle drug, and I would drink it like it was going out of style.

Once again, we don't need beer. We will, however, buy it because we want to live the kind of lifestyles and look like the people in the commercials do. That's why these types of commercials are made.

Now, some of you may be saying, "Hog wash! I don't buy it! There's no way these companies would do this!" You want to bet? Fact is, companies have been doing this for years. And they've been making millions of dollars in the process. Do you know why? Because it works, that's why.

If it didn't work, why would they keep running the same type of commercials year after year? Remember, it costs a lot of money to run a television commercial. If this approach didn't work, these companies would have gone bankrupt years ago. Are they bankrupt? No. Therefore, it has to work.

Now that we know this, I'm sure you all heard the saying, "If you can't beat them, join them." Well, that's exactly what you should do with your products and services. I highly recommend you sell your potential customers on what they will WANT from purchasing your products and services.

This doesn't mean you should lie to them. No. And it certainly doesn't mean you should totally delude them (like the T.V. commercials do) either! The companies who run these far fetched commercials take it too far! They consider it entertaining, and it is. However, it is very deluding.

In Network Marketing, it's different. Here's why: Yes, you do want to sell your people on what they will WANT from using your products and services. But you don't have to exaggerate any of the facts and figures. That's because the products and services which are represented in this industry really do help people and are, by far, the greatest on the market.

Now, I'm not saying that all the products and services on television do not help us. A few of them do. But let's face it, the majority of them are really not good for us. Therefore, these companies almost have to fabricate their stories just to get us to purchase their products and services. And as long as we keep buying, they'll keep doing it.

Of all the Network Marketing companies I know and deal with, I can honestly say that I don't know of one product or service that doesn't benefit the consumer in some way. I mean, this industry markets and promotes education, environmental products, nutrition, vitamins and weight loss, health care, family interaction programs, safety products

156

and services, skin care, excellent cleaning products, investment plans, telecommunications, travel discounts, etc. These are just a few. There are many more.

All of these products and services are extremely beneficial to all of us in numerous ways. Therefore, there's no need to over-exaggerate their potential. It's a win/win situation for all of us. We get to sell them on what they will WANT and also what they NEED. However, you should always focus more on what they WANT.

Knowing this, whatever products and services you represent, it's important for you to take the time to create at least 3 serious wants for each of them. It's imperative to know these things upfront. I recommend you do it right now! Remember: people don't need beer. But they do WANT to eat lobster and party with the "Swedish bikini team". People may not need your products and services right now, either. But if you create a serious WANT, they will not be able to resist. You know what I mean?

If you want to do well,

sell others what they

need.

If you want to get rich,

sell others what they

want.

22

After the Sale

Why would we even think about writing a chapter entitled "After The Sale" for this book? I mean, after the sale is made, we should thank the customer and move on to the next customer, right? What else could we possibly do for our new customer after the sale is made?

Believe it or not, this is how the majority of us think most of the time. Most of us figure, after the sale is made, the only logical thing to do is to move on to the next customer. Now, this thinking is not totally wrong, but it's no where near totally right, either! In other words, it's half right.

Yes, you do want to move on and share your products and services with the next person, but do you really think you should just forget about the person who just purchased from you? My answer to this question is - NO WAY!

The reason why most of us feel we should simply move on and forget about our previous customers is that's what always happened to us in the past after we purchased something. At least that's what always happened to me. The person who would sell me something would pretty much forget I existed a day or two after the sale was made. He/she would be real nice to me while the sale was being made, but after I'd leave, they would move on to the next customer and forget all about me.

Of course, I was never offended at the fact that they didn't keep in touch with me. I never expected them to. But what if they did? I don't know about you, but I would feel like they really cared about me and really wanted to make sure I was happy with my purchase. The reason why I know I would feel this way is because, not too long ago, it finally happened - I was treated like GOLD.

As you know, Network Marketing has been very good to me. It has enabled me to do things I only dreamed I could do. For instance, back in 1991, (a little over a year from the day I started in this great industry), I was able to purchase my first brand new vehicle. It was a Mercedes-Benz. Prior to this industry, I could never afford to drive a new vehicle. I always had to settle for pre-owned cars. In other words - used cars.

The reason for this story is, when I purchased my Mercedes, I was treated like a customer *should* be treated. During the sale, I was never pressured to buy. Ed (my salesperson) always made me feel like I was in control. This made me feel very comfortable.

After the purchase was final, I honestly didn't expect him to do anything else. *But he did!* He just kept doing and doing. He called me on the phone to see if everything was fine. He sent me "thank you" cards. He scheduled service appointments for me. He sent me personal invitations to the local Mercedes-Benz automobile shows. How could I not like this guy? The result? Everyone I know who is looking to buy a Mercedes-Benz gets sent to Ed.

If you think about it, I sort of work for Ed. He treated me right! Therefore, I (out of being a very satisfied customer) send everyone I know to him. I don't get paid to do this, mind you, I do it because I want to. Do you think Ed minds? No! As a matter of fact, he loves it! Wouldn't you?

Ed is a true 20%'er. How do I know? That's simple. He does all the things the 20%'ers do. He, like all 20%'ers, not only looks to make customers, he looks to make friends. And believe me, Ed always treated me like I was his friend. Whenever my car needed service, he always made sure I had a loaner vehicle ready just in case I needed one. And when he saw me at the Mercedes-Benz shows, he was always happy to see me. Again, all this was done after the sale was made. How could I not send my friends to him?

Most 20%'ers realize the customer doesn't expect any special treatment either before, during or after the sale. (I didn't say they don't WANT special treatment, I said they don't expect it!) They just want a little respect and a good deal. But if the sales person does go out of his/her way, especially after the sale is made, the customer will definitely know he/she truly cares about them. In fact, the customer will not only feel like they purchased a good product or service, but they also made a friend.

Most successful people in sales feel the most important part of the sale is actually after it's made. I agree. Obviously, making the sale first is very important. Without the sale, there would be no need to focus on what to do afterwards. However, after the sale is final, successful sales people will continue to do the things that really make the customers feel they purchased from the right company and from the right person. Just like Ed did to me.

And if the customer likes the product or service, likes the company and likes the salesperson, where do you think they will send their families and friends who are also interested and want to purchase it? You got it. They'll send them to the place and person they purchased from. And they'll do it not because they *have* to, but because they'll *want* to. *What a concept!*

161

This is exactly what you want to do! You should never forget about your customers after you make a sale. NEVER! Besides, keeping in touch with them (thank you cards, phone calls, holiday greeting cards, birthday cards, etc.) can and will be very profitable for you.

Once again, here's why - R E F E R R A L S ! ! !

Think about it, if you purchased something, and a friend of yours really liked it and wanted to purchase it also, and the person who sold it to you treated you right, would you refer your friend to him/her? Of course you would!

Now that you're on the other end, wouldn't you like your satisfied customers to send you tons of referrals? I would certainly hope so. Believe me, this is definitely what the 20%'ers do. And it's probably the most important thing they do differently than the 80%'ers. Referrals can account for up to 40% of their business. Again, they get these referrals because they treat their customers the way people should be treated - LIKE GOLD.

The bottom line is referrals are *KEY* for massive success without many added hours. What do I mean when I say, "without many added hours"? That's simple. When your satisfied customers send you referrals, it's almost a guaranteed sale. These people will already know about your products and services, the price, and most importantly, how great you are (thanks to your satisfied customer). Therefore, when they come to see you, or vice versa, they will be ready to do business.

A referral, in my opinion, is like receiving a gift from your satisfied customers. And believe me, when you get them, it's usually a quick and easy sale. Talk about an awesome exchange! You give them great service, and they'll send you great people. Hence, you'll make more sales "without many added hours". Makes sense, doesn't it?

Folks, I am convinced beyond a shadow of a doubt that if you just treat your customers the way 20%'ers do, *it'll work wonders in your life!* If you don't believe me, ask another 20%'er. They will undoubtedly agree with EVERYTHING I am sharing with you in this book from start to finish.

Now that you know this, you shouldn't keep this information a secret! It should be your duty to make sure everyone in your group reads it. Take it from a 20%'er, this sales approach will definitely help you reach the 20% plateau if you just apply it! It has worked for me and many, many other people who wanted to get ahead in sales, without taking advantage of the customer.

Now, if your satisfied customers do not send people your way, you should definitely ask for them. There is, however, a right way to do it. Here's how it should be done: After the sale is made, you want to either call your customers on the phone or send them a "thank you" card. Before you do, however, give them a couple of days to try out what they purchased.

When you do call or write, there are 3 things you should definitely cover. First, you want to make sure everything is okay with what they purchased. A lot of sales people dislike contacting their customers after the sale is made because they fear something may be wrong with what they purchased. Let's face it, things can go wrong from time to time. However, by contacting them, you can help fix whatever is wrong. When you do this, you will *again* go beyond what they expect of you. And believe me, they will love you for it.

Second, you want to once again thank them for their business. Face it, without customers, you're out of business!   Therefore, a *sincere* thank you is definitely in order.

Third, you want to know if they feel you truly HELPED them with their purchase.   Why do I emphasize the word *helped*?   Because it's now time to ask them for referrals.   And if they feel you HELPED them (not took advantage of them), they may know other people you can also HELP.   Therefore, ask them this question verbatim, "Is there anyone else you know who I can help?"   Most of the time, you'll get the answer you not only want, but deserve - *YES!*

In closing, remember: If you truly want to become a 20%'er, it all starts with a personal commitment.   After that, you have to CARE about everyone you come in contact with and treat every one of your customers as if they were your mother.   Then, you want to create a serious WANT for your products and services.   And finally, after the sale is made, you want to treat all the referrals you get the same way you treated your original customers - LIKE GOLD!   I challenge you to try this for awhile.   See where it takes you!   If done right, you will not be disappointed.   That's a promise from me to you.

Unused talents

give you no advantage

over someone who has

no talents at all.

Part Four

Building

For

the Future

Nothing

will run itself

unless it's running

downhill.

23

Building Your Business

The most important thing needed for building a successful distributorship in Network Marketing is not money, *it's people.* Let's face it, people make the world go around. And one thing God gave us plenty of in this world is people. Thank goodness for that. If you think about it, nothing down here would matter much without people.

For instance, think of money. Without people, money would be worthless. Dogs don't like money, nor do cats. In fact, besides people, there are no living beings on this planet who use money. And there are millions of them! Therefore, the most powerful commodity on earth is not money, it's people.

Now, when you're looking for people for your business, as we already stated earlier in the book, you are not limited to any one geographical area. It's open market for all of us! And once you find a person for your group, not only is he/she in your group, but so is everyone he/she finds, and so on and so forth.

If you do your research, you'll find there are not many companies/industries out there who allow their reps this kind of freedom. What they'll do instead is limit their reps by setting up and assigning territories. Sounds controlling, huh? With this industry, however, wherever your company goes, you can go too! Now that's what I call *freedom!*

Now let's talk about building your business. Most people, prior to signing up in this industry, feel they have to sign up 200-300 people in order to become successful. This statement is so far from the truth. If it was true, no one would be successful!

This business is not one person finding a lot of people. On the contrary, it's a lot of people finding a few *key* people each. What is a key person? A key person is simply a person who gets involved to win. He/she shares their products, services and opportunity on a continual basis. These people do not have to be convinced to do this business. They just do it. They are always attending the opportunity meetings and are always bringing new people with them. THEIR ATTITUDES REFLECT THEIR FUTURES - *AWESOME!*

Now that you know what a key person is, you need to realize and accept the fact that not everyone who signs up in your organization will be one. Some people in this industry expect all of their distributors to be key people. The result? They are constantly pushing, begging and convincing them to do this business. This is a huge mistake!

Think about it, if you owned your own multi-million dollar company, and you needed help with expansion, would you even consider hiring a person who you knew you'd have to beg or convince just to show up for work in the morning? No way! Have you ever heard the expression, "It's easier to give birth than it is to resurrect the dead"? Well, if you constantly have to convince someone to do this business, you may want to heed this advice and give birth to someone who is worthy of your time.

The bottom line is, *if you want to become successful in this industry, you have to surround yourself with the right people - KEY PEOPLE!* You can't force someone to become a key player, it's totally their choice. But you can choose who you want to work with. Therefore, if your new people want to succeed in Network Marketing, and they want you to spend quality time with them, they have to do what the key people do. If not, NEXT!

We are in the sorting business, not the begging and convincing business! If you constantly have to beg and convince the people in your group, you are not surrounding yourself with the right people. Hence, you're trying to resurrect the dead. And if you hang around with people who are dying, there's a good chance you will too.

When building this business, you're looking for the right people to help you complete your success puzzle. And like doing a puzzle, if you were looking for a certain piece, would you grab the first piece you could get your hands on and beg it or try to convince it to fit, even if it wasn't the right piece? No! That would make absolutely no sense at all. Instead, you would sort through the box until you found the right piece. That's what you have to do now.

This business is not for everyone! In fact, most people you meet will not get involved. Thank goodness for that. If they did, this would no longer be an opportunity. However, because God was nice enough to fill the earth with billions and billions of people, there are still countless millions of people out there who will get involved and will be key players. How many of them do you want in your group?

Let's say you're looking to find 5 key people: If this is the case, you may have to sign up 30, 40 or even 50 people to find them. Others may have to sign up more! Regardless of how many it will take, I can assure you it will be well worth your while to do so.

By the way, this doesn't mean that after you find 5 key people, you should stop looking. No, that would be a major mistake. You should always be looking for new blood. Believe it or not, even successful distributorships can stagnate without constant growth. Why? Because new, excited distributors are what make this industry tick. It's true. Without them, we'd be doing the same thing over and over every day with the same people. You know, like a job.

This is not only true in Network Marketing, it's true in almost every industry. Let's look at professional sports. Every year, they have what is known as the professional draft. In this draft, every team gets to select new players. You don't see any teams bypassing this draft, not even the world champions! That's because all teams want to get better. And the best way to get better and build for the future is to get new talent (new blood).

Here's another example: Picture a church. What would happen to the church's momentum if the same exact people showed up each and every week? Do you think the Pastor of the church would give his very best week in and week out for the same people? Probably not. However, what would happen if just one new person walked into that church, someone who really wanted to be there? *You got it!* A revival would take place! One new person would jump start the whole church and get everyone going again, especially the Pastor.

Now, if one new, enthusiastic person can revive a church, what could one new person do for your group? I can tell you from experience that one person can turn your whole business around. That's why, even after you find your 5 key people, it's imperative for you to avoid stagnation by constantly being on the lookout for more.

Now, there are 4 major recruiting approaches you can use when building your business. These 4 approaches will help you find all the people you want, if you're willing to work for it. There are other approaches, of course, but let's just focus on these four because they are, by far, the most effective. The 4 approaches I'm referring to are:

1) Warm Market

2) Contacts

3) Advertising

4) Video Pass Out

In the next 4 chapters, we're going to break these 4 approaches down for you. This way, you can see for yourself just how powerful they really are. So without further delay, let's get busy.

No man

can become rich

without himself

enriching others.

24

Approach #1 - Warm Market

If you're going to build a large group of distributors, the first approach I recommend you take is to utilize your *warm market* contacts. Warm market contacts are simply people you know personally and are comfortable with. They could be your family members, friends, neighbors, work mates, former work mates, fellow church members, your doctor, lawyer, etc. In other words, your warm market is all the people you know and care about and would love to work with, but never had the chance to due to having different professions.

Think about it, you are now in a business where you can actually build something for yourself, while working with your *family* and *friends*. *Isn't that incredible?!* Families can actually build something together in this industry. In my opinion, this is the greatest asset of Network Marketing.

The thing that blows my mind the most, however, is the person who gets involved and doesn't want to share this life-changing opportunity with his/her family and friends. They say they want to wait and see if they can become successful first, before actually sharing it with anyone they know. *To each his own.*

I can honestly say that the people I know who are truly successful in this industry all have their family members and friends involved with them. These distributors all cared enough about their loved ones to share this incredible opportunity with them. Looking back, that's all I did. I made a list of everyone I could think of. Then I got busy sharing my opportunity with them.

You need to do the same thing also! It all starts with you making a list of everyone you know. Then, you want to share your opportunity with every one of them. Remember - CARING IS SHARING. (When making your list, one thing I recommend you do is to think of everyone who knows you. For some reason, when we try to think of everyone we know, we don't even know where to start. This overwhelms us. But when we think of the people who know us, the names just keep on coming. So, by doing this, you'll think of many more names.)

The more belief you have in your business, the more you'll want to share it with your warm market contacts. My motto is: *If it's good enough for you, it's good enough for them.* Most people are afraid to share this opportunity with their family and friends because of a fear of rejection. Fact is, some of your family members and friends will see the opportunity, and some won't. But if you don't share it with them, you'll never know.

Pre Judging

After making your list of warm market contacts, DO NOT pre-judge anyone! Learn from my mistake. I did this more than once, and it cost me dearly. Here's an example: A friend of mine named Mike was a bartender at a Ground Round restaurant. He is a very dynamic individual. Besides tending bar, Mike also did television commercials. With his hectic schedule, I thought he'd be far too busy to get involved in this industry. Boy was I wrong!

He did get involved. Further, he was with the same company I was involved with. He started 5

176

months after I did. I couldn't believe it! I did have him on my list, but I never shared the opportunity with him. The bottom line is - I prejudged him. This foolishness cost me a dynamic distributor. The person who did sign Mike up barely knew him. Mike should have been in my group. But due to my prejudging him, I lost him. This experience taught me a big, big lesson.

Once again, you'll never know whether or not the person on your list will ever become successful if you don't share this opportunity with them. If you don't share it with them, one of two things will happen; either someone else will (like my experience with Mike), or no one will. And if that's the case, they will never know how powerful Network Marketing really is. Either way, you lose.

Now let's get back to prejudging. Let's say you got involved, made your list and started sharing this opportunity with your warm market contacts. On your list was your friend Steve. Every time you looked at your list of potential distributors, you always overlooked Steve.

You knew Steve had talent and could easily excel in Network Marketing (because of his success in Corporate America). But every time you saw his name, you would say, "Steve would be great, but he is far too busy and far too successful to even listen to me." And with this thought in mind, you never attempted to share your opportunity with him.

As time went on, you started to become very successful. As a matter of fact, in just one year's time, you had a distributorship which spanned all over the country. It got so big that you were forced to travel all over the country to help train them all.

One day, as you were returning home from one of your trips, your spouse was waiting for you at the airport. He/she had a limousine awaiting your arrival. After landing, the two of you were chauffeured to your favorite restaurant. Once you entered the restaurant, your table was already awaiting you. You were seated immediately, and there was a bottle of champagne on ice waiting for you.

During the meal, all you kept talking about was how incredible your trip was. "More people showed up for the training than we had expected, and nearly everyone is making money," you told your spouse. You then continued, "I even managed to recruit two flight attendants and a baggage check-in clerk on my flight home."

Everything just happened to be going your way.

Just as you finished talking, one of the waiters walked by your table. To your surprise, it was your friend Steve. When Steve saw you, he had to look twice. He just couldn't believe how great the two of you looked.

Steve was absolutely blown away when he heard how successful you had become over the past year. When he asked how you did it, you replied, "I started my own Network Marketing business. It's a business where anyone can become successful if they're willing to work hard and believe in themselves. That's all I did." You then asked, "By the way Steve, what in the world are you doing working here?"

Steve told you that due to changing times, he lost his job. He said there were no other companies out there who would start him off at the same salary he had been previously earning. After seven months of unemployment, he really needed the money. He had to do something fast. That's why he became a waiter.

Steve then asked you, "You said anyone could do this Network Marketing business, right?" "Why, yes!" you replied. Upset, he asked, "I thought we were friends? I have been going broke for seven months, and you didn't even let me know about your new business? Friends don't do things like that." After that, he walked away in disgust.

If this happened to you, would you want to eat your meal? I wouldn't either.

On the other hand, if you didn't prejudge him, and you did share your opportunity with him, would you be able to eat your meal then? Sure you would. You could then say, "Steve, do you remember the opportunity I shared with you last year? Well, it paid off." If this was the case, regardless of whether or not Steve saw the opportunity, at least you would have done your part and shared it with him. Therefore, you wouldn't need to feel guilty. You would feel bad for Steve, but not guilty. Because, once again, at least you *cared* enough about him to share it with him.

In short, if you don't share your opportunity with your family and friends, you'll never know if it is or is not for them. Face it, even if they don't see it, they are still your family and still your friends. They're not going to disown you for sharing something with them. The worst case scenario will be for them to say, "No thanks" or "It's not for me." That's it. You'll still watch football games together and go to the movies together. You just won't be working together.

Therefore, SHARE YOUR OPPORTUNITY WITH THEM! This business just may change their lives like it has yours. But if you don't share it with them, you'll never know. Remember - *Caring is sharing. If it's good enough for you, it's good enough for them.*

The

only thing you get

without working

is hungry.

25

Approach #2 - Contacts

The second approach I recommend is *contacts*. Contacts are the people you know, but are not real close with. They can be people you know from doing business with in the past or they can be people you are referred to. In addition, contacts are also the new people you meet every day in restaurants, airports, malls, business card exchanges, clubs, etc. Truly, *everywhere* you go and *everyone* you meet is a new contact to you.

Before you go crazy meeting new contacts, however, I recommend you first make another list. This list should be of all the contacts you know (that were made throughout your life). One way for you to remember some of your contacts is to look for all the business cards you have collected over the years. I recruited a few people this way.

For instance, I had this one contact who was in the insurance business. I have to admit I totally forgot about him until I found his business card. Sadly for me, even after I did find his card, I still pre-judged him at first. However, after the incident with my friend Mike, I decided to never prejudge anyone ever again.

When I finally did call Bob (my insurance contact), he agreed to meet with me, but he didn't really see an opportunity. However, before we parted, I asked him this, "Bob, who do you know who would be interested in seeing this opportunity?"

After that, I kept quiet and he led me to Jeffrey Bouton.

Jeffrey, like Bob, was also in the insurance business. Jeffrey is from Indiana, Pa. After seeing the opportunity presentation, he signed up immediately. Further, he opened up his own office. This really excited me because I now had someone in my group open up an office in a part of the country I had never before heard of. Jeffrey was a natural for this business!

My point for this story is, if I would have totally prejudged Bob (my original contact), I would have never found Jeffrey. SO, EVEN IF YOU DON'T THINK YOUR CONTACT WILL DO THIS BUSINESS, SHOW IT TO HIM/HER ANYWAY! Because even if they don't see it, they may lead you to someone who will. However, if you don't ask, you'll never know. Remember - *Who do you know? Who do you know? Who do you know?*

There are many great contact stories I can tell you. Here is a *new contact* story. One night after a meeting, I went to a Bennigan's restaurant with a few of my friends. Our waitress was a friendly gal. Her name was Cindy.

After talking to her for awhile, I let her know my company was looking for a few part-time people to help us in our expansion. I didn't mention getting rich or starting her own business. That probably would have scared her. Instead, I mentioned only part-time work. I told her part-time people were working an extra 10 hours a week and earning anywhere from $400 - $500 a month.

She then told me that both she and her fiance, Tom, were looking for part-time work. They were planning to get married, but money was tight. I didn't try to explain the business to her. All I did was talk about the person who was going to do the presentation. I said that he was the one who was looking for people, not me. I told her I couldn't explain it even if I tried. She agreed to bring Tom to the meeting on Thursday to see what was going on.

The night of the meeting, not only did Tom and Cindy come, but so did Cindy's mother! As it turned out, Cindy and her mother did not see an opportunity. Tom, on the other hand, hit the roof! He saw it immediately! Tom, like Jeffrey, was also a natural.

Tom was brought up in a successful business environment, and it showed. He is one of the most successful people I've ever met! After Tom got involved, his business expanded all over the country in only a few months. His business talents, combined with his great attitude were the main reasons for him finding the caliber of people he did.

I never knew Tom prior to doing this business. I would have never met him either, had I not spoken to Cindy (now his wife), when she was a waitress at Bennigan's. This is just further proof that things may seem small at first, but in time, can develop into something huge. Think about it, a conversation with a waitress turned into me finding one of the most dynamic people I had ever met! Once again, Tom didn't get involved from me mentioning getting rich or owning a business, it all stemmed from part-time work.

Mention Part-Time Work First

Think about this, if you were approached by someone (especially someone you didn't know), who told you you could become a millionaire in 2 years, would you believe him/her? Probably not. Most of us would run away from that person as fast as we could! This is the biggest mistake we can make when it comes to recruiting people into our businesses. When we mention $10,000 a month or financial independence, we scare most people. Therefore, my advice is to mention only part-time work to these people.

If you mention $400 - $500 a month to these people, and after showing up, they find out the earning potential is much higher, this will excite them! This is called *under promising* and *over delivering*. On the other hand, if you tell someone they can earn $10,000 a month, and after showing up, they find out they can only earn $400 - $500 a month, this will discourage them.

Now, there are those rare individuals you'll meet who are used to dealing with big numbers. These people don't want to hear about $400 - $500 a month. They will want to know upfront the full potential your opportunity offers. My advice is to let them know that the sky is the limit. But don't try to explain everything to them. Just give them enough information to excite them. Then, when they come to the meeting, they'll get to see firsthand how powerful the opportunity really is. For most of the people you meet, however, just mention part-time work.

Being The Right Person

One more thing: When looking for people, the main thing is not *finding* the right person, it's *being* the right person. If we're out there meeting people, and our egos are out of control, who would want to work with us? I know I wouldn't want to work with us! Most people don't like working with those who think they are the deal. I know I don't. Therefore, the one thing we should never make an issue of when we are looking for people is ourselves. We should talk highly of everything else - the company, the training, the products and services, the person doing the presentation - just not ourselves.

If you think about it, that's what I did with Cindy. I talked highly of everything except myself. You should too! When you humble yourself and take no credit, you will find the right person. That's because you'll be acting like the right person. The bottom line is, if you brag about yourself, they will want to come in to see you. On the other hand, if you brag about the opportunity (and not yourself), they will want to come in to see it! Which one will make you more money? You don't have to be a rocket scientist to figure that one out.

Anything

that is worth doing

is worth doing

well.

26

Approach #3 - Advertising

The third approach I recommend is *advertising*. Advertising can be done in newspapers, magazines, flyers, computers, radio, television, etc. The reason for advertising is to find the people you would never get to meet otherwise. Some people start advertising immediately after getting involved. Others never advertise at all. When I first started, I didn't advertise for the first 2 months. I didn't need to! I was too busy getting my family, friends and contacts involved.

After I did start advertising, however, I found it to be a very lucrative way to go. It enabled me to find a lot of great people I would never have met otherwise. I personally know advertising works because that's how I got started in this industry.

Prior to Network Marketing, as you know by now, I was in business with my twin brother Mike. We both worked real hard, but we could never make ends meet. Besides that, I was miserable. I hated my business! I hated the fact that I was always within a 5 mile radius of my business 90% of my life. It just seemed like every day was the same old thing. To make things worse, not only were we both miserable, we were both broke! This craziness went on for months.

One day, as I was reading the newspaper, I saw an advertisement in the "Help Wanted" section regarding starting a business which could involve traveling. It sounded very interesting, so I called. I was honestly calling just to hear what it was about. After hearing a few facts and figures, I left a message on the machine and asked for more information. Four days later, I received a return phone call. After hearing more about the company, I decided to go in and check it out. And, as they say, the rest is history!

Reach the Masses

Advertising in newspapers, magazines, flyers, catalogs, information super highway, etc., today is a very powerful way to reach the masses and find key people for your business. With persistence, it can be very lucrative for you. One thing I know for sure is that it's much easier finding people from advertising today than it was back in 1989. Why? Because back in 1989, the economy was still in decent shape, and the job market appeared to be secure. Today, however, the country is in shambles! Everyone is looking for work, but no one is hiring.

There are so many unemployed, yet very talented individuals out there who are searching for an opportunity, one that can change their current situation and offer them future stability. These individuals are tired of being laid off yearly. In a sense, the economy being so bad is an advantage for us. These people are now forced into being more open minded because nothing else out there is working.

Once they see the power of our industry and the income potential it offers, they will also get excited like you and I did when we started. Most of these individuals (after signing up) will start off part time while they continue to search for a job in their field. However, once they actually see the positive results of this business, they are in for life.

Advertising is definitely a great tool for the distributor who has just relocated to a new part of the country and doesn't know many or any people. I can definitely relate to this.

Whenever we would expand to a new part of the country, I would always fly out there to help get things off the ground. Some of these locations were in cities/towns I had never been before. Therefore, I was forced to advertise. Of course, I met contacts everywhere I went, but advertising was definitely my main source of finding people.

I found some of my best people through running ads in the newspaper. And every time I found a new person, I also found a new warm market - THEIRS! After they would sign up, we would talk to their families, friends and contacts. Think about it, they would bring their families, friends and contacts to me, and I would train them. I repeated this process everywhere I went! It was a win-win situation for all of us.

Once again, advertising reaches the masses. When corporate companies are looking for people, they put "Help Wanted" ads in the newspaper. You're also looking for good people for your company. One way to get your message out is through advertising. When people are looking for a job or an opportunity, where do most of them look? They look through the newspaper, right? Sure they do.

Quality Prospects

As I mentioned before, some of the best people I found came from ads in the newspaper. I met actors/actresses who needed part-time work. I met bored millionaires. I met airline pilots. I met retired professional athletes, and so on. Again, I would never have met these great people had I not put an ad in the paper.

The quality of people you will attract will be based upon the type of ads you run. So make sure you put some thought into them. If you want to attract people like yourself, design an ad that you would respond to. If you want a top-notch executive, design your ad that way. If you want your phone to ring off the hook, run a generalized ad or part-time ad. If you want less calls, but better quality calls, create an ad which will attract quality prospects. I recommend you run all types of ads. This way you'll have a nice blend of people in your group.

When I first started to advertise, all I wanted to do was recruit the big-time executives. However, in time, I realized the fact that part-time people also know potential superstars. So I started to run part-time ads too. These part-time people led me to some of the most incredible people I ever met! *TALK ABOUT AWESOME!*

This business is not one person doing a lot, it's a lot of people doing a little. Therefore, it's not the person who responds to your ad who will make the real difference in your group, it's who he/she knows.

In short, advertising allows us to find the people we would never have met otherwise. If we treat them right, they'll treat us right. They'll introduce us to everyone they know. What a concept!

So, if you're a person who either doesn't know many people or who has relocated to a new area, no more excuses! Advertising will help you find the people who do have families and friends you can contact. In other words, if you don't have your own family and friends to contact, this approach will help you find someone who does.

190

I can state with confidence this approach works. *First*, because of the people I found through advertising, and *second*, because that's how I got started in Network Marketing. *TRY IT. YOU'LL LIKE IT!*

There is one thing I need to stress: NEVER MISLEAD ANYONE! Do not create false ads to lure people in. If you do, you're not only hurting yourself, you're hurting the whole industry. That will not make us fellow networkers very happy. There is an old adage in radio broadcasting that says: Keep the airwaves sacred. If and when you advertise, you need to do the same thing. Keep the newspapers sacred! Create an honest ad and be honest with everyone who responds to it. If you can't do this - DON'T ADVERTISE!

Weak men

wait for opportunities.

Strong men

make them.

27

Approach #4 - Video Pass-out

Video pass-out is such a powerful tool for us in this industry. It allows us to have presentations in the homes of our prospects, without us actually having to do them or be there ourselves. This is a great tool, especially for the new people who don't know how to do a presentation yet.

Think about it, with this approach, all you have to do is give your prospects a video tape which will explain the company you represent and the opportunity available. *It's that simple!* If after seeing the video, they see an opportunity, the next step is to get them to a live opportunity presentation.

For those of us who get real nervous when it comes time to recruiting, video pass-out will definitely help to overcome this. That's because video tapes don't get nervous, only people do! The VCR will not shake like a leaf once the video is put into it. Not a chance. Instead, it will create magic. Face it, all video tapes look the same when they're not playing. But once you put your video into their VCR and push play, your company video will turn their television into a magic screen full of possibilities. At least that's how I see it.

Another reason why video pass-out is so powerful today is that it's so convenient. A lot of people today cannot go to a meeting due to lack of time. If they work one job, it's usually 50-60 hours a week. If they don't have a full-time job, they probably have 2 to 3 part-time jobs. *Talk about ridiculous!* It's not their fault, however. Once again, it's the *system.*

The little bit of free time these people do have is used to relax and spend time with their families. These people will be too tired to come to a meeting to hear a one-hour presentation. They will, however, watch a 20-minute video in their own home.

The greatest thing about video pass-out is *anyone can do it!* With this approach, an 18 year old teenager can easily recruit a 50 year old executive into his/her business. That's because the executive will not be focused on the teenager; he/she will be focused on the video. The bottom line is, the video will flat out add much more credibility than the teenager ever could.

Now, if after viewing the tape, the executive is still interested and wants to know more about the opportunity available, all the teenager would need to do at this point is plug the executive into a meeting where he/she can talk to the top people in the company. Then, when the executive gets involved, who's group will he/she be in? *You got it!* The teenager's group. *It's an unbelievable concept!*

Opportunity videos are also tremendous for the people you know who live far away from you. For instance, if you live in Phoenix, and you have a friend who lives in Detroit, all you would have to do is send him/her a company video along with some paperwork on your company. (We'll be discussing the paperwork shortly.)

Now, before sending the video tape and information, try not to explain too much of the opportunity to them. Let them know that everything will be explained to them (in the video) better than you could ever hope to explain it. This will get you off the hook. Fact is, most Network

194

Marketing companies produce extraordinary videos which will wet their appetites better than we can. Therefore, my advice to you is to let the video tape do the explaining. This is a very powerful, professional approach.

By the way, this approach is not only used in our industry, it's used in the franchise industry also. If you were interested in starting your own franchise, most companies would send you a video tape and some information to familiarize you with their concept. Now if this approach didn't work, why would major franchises use it? The truth is - *it really does work.*

You need to know that there is an art to handing out video tapes. Once you master it, success will be yours. There are 4 steps to video pass-out. Some people learn to master these 4 steps, while others take short cuts and blow it. When done right, this 4-step approach will definitely deliver you the results you want. Therefore, I highly recommend you learn and utilize it as soon as possible. So, without further delay, let's get busy.

The First Step

The first step to video pass-out is to either call your prospects on the phone or stop by their home with your video tape. When speaking with them, always show *excitement* and *urgency*. If you're going to tell them this is the greatest opportunity in the world, you better be excited! If you are not enthused about your opportunity, don't expect your prospects to be either.

The reason why you want to show urgency is for fear of loss. When you're about to leave a video with your prospects, make sure they are definitely going to watch it that day/night, or don't leave it. Say to them something like, "I only have a few video tapes, and I have a lot of people to share this opportunity with." Then ask them, "Are you definitely going to watch it tonight? If not, I can't leave it. I'll have to bring it back later." When you do this, your prospects will feel a fear of loss, and they will *make the time* to watch the video.

DO NOT leave them a video tape only. Most people don't believe everything they see, but nearly everyone believes what they read. (For instance, when buying a new car, the salesperson will tell us all about the vehicle and its features, and we may or may not believe him/her. But after we read about it in the owner's manual, we believe it to be true). Therefore, besides the video, give them as much *positive paperwork* on both the *company* you represent and the *industry* as you can.

I never used to include paperwork when passing out video tapes. I still got good results. However, once I added the paperwork, the positive results increased tremendously. Including paperwork with the video tape is just plain smart! First of all, it's definitely a more professional approach (than not adding it). Second, it will add more credibility to both your company and the industry. Third, your results will increase BIG TIME!

Now, after you give them the video tape and paperwork, let them know you'll be back *tomorrow* to pick it up. Again, this will show urgency. The absolute worst thing you can do after giving them your video tape would be to say, "Oh, take your time, I don't really need it back." If you do this, there is a good chance they won't even watch it.

There's no urgency or fear of loss behind that statement. There's no deadline. So believe me, most of them will take their good old time. On the other hand, when you tell them you'll be back tomorrow to pick it up, they are now against the clock. The more persuasive you are with them, the better your results will be.

That's all there is to the first step. Once again, all you have to do is drop off the video tape and paperwork to your prospects and show enthusiasm and urgency while doing it. Did you notice I didn't mention anything about the products and services yet? That's part of the second step.

The Second Step

The second step to video pass-out starts off with a phone call. It's vital for you to call them the very next day! If your prospects are hot for the deal, you don't want to give them a chance to cool down. It's like if you have a boiling pot of water on the stove, and you turn the burner off. What will happen to the water? It will eventually cool down, right? That's what can happen to your prospects also. The more time you give them to think it over, the colder they will get.

Therefore, you need to call them the very next day. Even if they don't see an opportunity, it's still good to call the very next day. Face it, you'll need to get your video tape and information back immediately so you can share it with someone else, right?

Once you get your prospects on the phone, the conversation should be short and sweet. There will be no need for you to beat around the bush. They will know why you're calling. Therefore, after saying hello, simply ask them if they watched the video tape last night. That's all there is to it!

After they answer you, ask them if they enjoyed it! If they did, ask them this, "Which part of the video did you like most?" This question usually catches them off guard. My advice to you is to ask this question verbatim. Then, don't say another word - *just listen.* After they answer that question, ask them this: "Are you up for more training?" This is a simple *"yes"* or *"no"* question. (By the way, don't ask these questions to the ones who are not interested in your opportunity, only the ones who are).

When the people who do see an opportunity answer *"yes"* to this question, say, "Great, I am going to drop off another training video and more information for you tonight. What time will you be home?" Again, a friendly but direct question.

If they can't watch the training video that night, let them tell you they can't. In other words, never assume it yourself. Never ask, "Is it possible for you to see the training video tonight?" If you do, you're giving them an option. Direct questions usually get direct answers. If they can't see the training video that night, it's important for you to get them to see it as soon as possible.

After you set the appointment with them, there is still one more question you need to ask them. Here it is, "When I come over tonight/tomorrow, would you like me to bring some of the products and services with me?" Let them know you will be bringing them free samples (if possible). Who is going to say *"no"* to this question? No one in their right mind will.

Once again, the questions you'll be asking during the phone conversation are:

1) *Did you watch the video last night?*
2) *Which part of the video did you like most?*
3) *Are you up for more training?*

4) What time will you be home
tonight/tomorrow?
5) Would you like to see/try the
products and services?

The second-step information, like I already mentioned, should include another tape. Either a company training tape or a Network Marketing training tape (which we have available) will be fine. Along with the video tape, make sure you include more paperwork. What I would do here is include an application and other bits of information which will assume he/she is going to sign up.

Most importantly, don't forget to bring your products and services with you! Once they actually see them, if they like them, you'll have another customer/distributor.

By the way, unlike the first step, I do recommend you watch this video tape with them. Of course, when the tape is on, *get excited!* Even if you saw it 50 times before, it doesn't matter. Your excitement (or lack of it) will have a major effect on them. Remember, it's their first time watching it. Therefore, they will be impressionable. In other words, if you're excited, you can actually sway them in your direction.

Now, after watching the video and sharing your products and services with them, it's now time for the third step.

The Third Step

The third step to video pass-out is to get them to a live presentation. At this point, you should have a very excited person on your hands. These people are the best ones in attendance because they already know what they're coming to see. Most people who

199

come to see the presentation for the first time usually have little or no clue as to why they are there. Your new person, however, has already seen 2 video tapes and has read a lot of information on both the company and the industry. Therefore, he/she will be more comfortable than the other new people.

When your new people see and meet the quality of people who are already involved, this will pump them up even more! Before and after the meeting, make sure you introduce your new guests to everyone! This will help to make them feel even more comfortable and welcome. The key thing here is to make your new guests feel as if they are already part of the family.

The neatest thing about the third step is, once your people arrive, your job is pretty much done. The speaker/s will do the rest. You just have to sit back and watch things happen.

After the meeting is over, it's now time for them (your new guests) to commit to you! At this point, you did everything you should have done to properly present your company. It's now their turn. Most of the time, you won't have to say a word, they will tell you they're ready to get started and ready to order inventory. If they don't, however, it's up to you to ask.

Remember - time is money, and you do (or will) have other distributors in your group who will also need your time. The bottom line is: *FRIENDS ARE FRIENDS, FAMILY IS FAMILY, AND BUSINESS IS BUSINESS!* At this point, it's definitely time to do business. Again, you did your part. It's now their turn.

Now, if they're not quite ready yet, that's okay, too. Let them go at their own pace. Just don't let them slow you down! If you're building a large group, you should be working with more than one person at a time (either your people or your people's people). Therefore, you really will not have all the time in the world to spend with them.

Even if you did, however, I still recommend you don't. If you spend all of your time with them, they will know you're not building a business. How could you be? You're always with them! They will then question your commitment and/or ability to do this business. Or, they'll think you really need them in order to succeed. Otherwise, you wouldn't be spending so much of your time with them.

However, if they're not quite ready yet, this doesn't mean you should be mean or rude to them. They may want to research the company or see another presentation before totally committing. That's okay. For most of them, this will be their first business venture, and they may be a bit nervous. The best thing you can do for them at this point is to let them do what they have to do. However, you should always assure them that you will be there for them if and when they need you.

Now, once they do commit, you need to train them to do their own thing immediately. Train them to do everything you're doing with your business. Your goal is to get them to the point where they will no longer need you. This is very important for you because it will free up your schedule so you can find another person. I am not saying you should totally disconnect yourself from them (you should always be there for them), but it's their business. Therefore, they will need to step up and take control themselves.

The Fourth Step

The fourth step to video pass-out is to *duplicate this system with your newly signed distributors!* Believe me, after they get involved, they'll want to hand out video tapes to their contacts too! New distributors especially like the video pass-out approach. That's because it's the simplest approach. Therefore, make sure you teach it to them! Further, if you used this approach on them, let them know you did. This will help them see just how effective it really is.

Take Advantage of Video Pass-out

As you know, everyone has to see/hear a presentation prior to getting involved, whether it's a live meeting, a conference call, satellite, computer (information highway), a cassette tape or a video tape. Obviously, the more presentations you have going on, the more success you'll have. In my opinion, the **best** way for you to have a lot of presentations going on is through video pass-out. That's because with video pass-out it's possible for you to be in 2 places at the same time.

Here's an example: Let's say you handed out 3 videos this week. Out of the 3 people you gave a video tape to, 1 saw an opportunity and signed up. He/she committed to hand out 3 videos weekly also. How many video presentations would be going on in your group now? Six - 3 from you, and 3 from him/her.

Out of these 6 video presentations, let's say you both signed up 1 person each. These new distributors also committed to hand out 3 video tapes each week. How many video presentations would be going on now? Right, 12! How many of them did you hand out personally? Three. Now, can you see why you want to share this with your newly signed distributors?

Some distributors want to keep this approach all to themselves. This doesn't make any sense to me! You're looking to build a large group, right? Well then, you're going to need a lot of help. Do you think you could personally hand out 300 video tapes each week yourself? Not a chance! However, do you think you and 99 people in your organization could all hand out 3 video tapes each? Definitely! That's how you become wealthy!

Ray Kroc was the founder of McDonald's. He franchised his idea to anyone who wanted to be in business for themselves. Whenever Ray found a better way to do something, or if he had a new concept, he shared it with all of his franchisees. By helping them, he helped himself!

This is exactly what you want to do with the people in your group. When you have a new concept (video pass-out), don't keep it to yourself. Share it with everyone! By helping them, like Ray Kroc did, you'll be helping yourself!

Well, there you have it, the 4 steps to video pass-out. Remember, this business is not you finding a lot of people yourself, it's a lot of people finding a few good people each. Clearly, video pass-out is an awesome recruiting tool! It's definitely the most non-threatening, simplistic approach that you and the people in your group should use when building your businesses.

Once again, the 4 steps to video pass-out are:

1) Either *call* or *drop off a video tape* and some information to your prospects. Make sure you're excited and *always* show urgency.

2) If they see an opportunity, drop off another video tape with *more information* and let them try your *products* and *services.*

3) Get them to a *live presentation* and then get them to commit to the business.

4) *Duplicate* this approach with your new distributors.

This approach is very simple. *My advice is -* KEEP IT THAT WAY!

Now that we know the *4 key recruiting approaches* and how to immediately implement them, what type of people should we be looking for? The answer is simple. We are looking for people who are *as good* or *better* than us. This is called *recruiting up!*

The neat thing about life

is not so much

where you stand today,

as in what direction

you are moving.

28

Recruiting Up

Recruiting up is a slang expression used in Network Marketing which simply means "finding people better than ourselves." Since we're going to be sharing our opportunity with other people, don't you feel they should be good people? I would certainly hope so.

Did you know you can sign up 4,000 people in one year and still go broke? Sure, if you sign up 4,000 worthless people, expect worthless results. Therefore, it's important for you to remember: *it's not the quantity of the people you find, it's the quality of the people who will make the biggest difference for you in your business.*

Recruiting up works as follows: First, you need to honestly rate yourself on a scale from 1 to 10. You should rate yourself on attitude, ability, desire, leadership, experience, image and responsibility (Use chart at end of chapter). When doing this, you have to be honest! After you rate yourself on all of these categories, add up the numbers and divide it by 7 (the number of categories you rated yourself on). This will be your true number. After you do this, don't tell anyone; keep it to yourself. It's now time to get busy building your business. If (as an example) you rate yourself a 5, you're now looking for 6's, 7's or better.

This is where most people make their mistake. Instead of finding people who are better than themselves, they'll find a bunch of 1's and 2's and then wonder why their business is lacking. It's not lacking because this industry is about to go under (that will never happen!). It's lacking because of the people they're attracting.

Here's an example to illustrate the power of recruiting up vs. recruiting down:

	Recruiting Up	# of People	Recruiting Down
YOU	5	1	5
1st Generation	6's	5	4's
2nd Generation	7's	25	3's
3rd Generation	8's	125	2's
4th Generation	9's	625	1's
5th Generation	10's	3125	0's

It's amazing what the right people can do, as compared to the wrong people. Face it, we all know 1's, and we all know 10's. It's easy to share the opportunity with 1's. They'll listen to anything! There's no challenge to it. But when you do challenge yourself, and you share your opportunity with people who are 7's, 8's, 9's and 10's, your business will explode! These people will have a major impact on your life.

How will you know who is a 7, 8 or better? Good question. Well, first of all, you need to honestly rate them like you did yourself. Then, you need to ask yourself, "If this person gets involved, will he/she have a positive impact on my business?" If the answer is "Yes," that's the very first/next person you want to contact. Then, when you're finished with that person, take out your list and look for the next best qualified person, and so on.

Now, this doesn't mean you shouldn't sign a person up because he/she is a 3. No. Everyone deserves a fair chance in this industry! With proper training, 3's can develop into 7's, 8's, 9's and 10's.

Even if they don't, who do they know? They may know someone who is a 10. Therefore, give everyone a fair chance. When you treat people right, they can (and will) lead you to the people who can really have a major impact in your life.

In short, we're looking for the people who we feel are better than we are. We then want to train them to find people (for themselves) who are better than they are. Once again, let's not turn anyone away because he/she is a 3. That 3 may know a 4 who knows a 5 and so on. But let's not focus on the 3's, let's focus on the 8's, 9's and 10's. Finding enough 3's and 4's will eventually lead us to success, but why prolong it? Let's find the right people now!

PERSONAL RATING CHART

YOUR QUALITIES   YOUR RATING

(Circle 1 number for each category)

YOUR QUALITIES	YOUR RATING
ATTITUDE	1 2 3 4 5 6 7 8 9 10
ABILITY	1 2 3 4 5 6 7 8 9 10
DESIRE	1 2 3 4 5 6 7 8 9 10
LEADERSHIP	1 2 3 4 5 6 7 8 9 10
EXPERIENCE	1 2 3 4 5 6 7 8 9 10
IMAGE	1 2 3 4 5 6 7 8 9 10
RESPONSIBILITY	1 2 3 4 5 6 7 8 9 10

SUB-TOTAL - _____

DIVIDE BY 7 - _____

TOTAL PERSONAL RATING - _____

Success comes in

cans;

failure comes in

can'ts.

29

Trust vs. Respect = Success

Let's say you had a cavity, and you needed dental work done immediately. You were looking for a good dentist, and a friend of yours just happened to know one. He/she offered to set up an appointment for you. Would you go? Of course you would! You would go because you would trust him/her enough to take their advice, right?

Now, if he/she couldn't get an appointment for you for that day, would you let him/her do the dental work instead of the dentist? No way! You would *trust* him/her enough to take their advice, but you wouldn't *respect* his/her knowledge in dentistry. How could you? He's/she's not even a dentist!

The same applies to your Network Marketing business. Your family, friends and contacts will *trust* you enough to attend an opportunity meeting, but they are not going to *respect* your business sense in this industry, especially if you're new or part time. How could they? They know you're new. They also know you're probably not that successful yet.

On the other hand, they're not going to *trust* the speaker, but they will *respect* his/her business sense enough to listen to what he/she has to say. It's true! Your family, friends and contacts will attend the meeting because they *trust* you, but they're going to stay because they *respect* the speaker. That's what the *trust* - *respect* scenario is all about. This is very powerful!!!

Those who follow this scenario always seem to succeed. Those who don't always seem to fail. The ones who don't follow it, usually let their egos get in the way of their success. My advice is to control your ego. Don't worry about your prospects not respecting your business sense. The key thing here is to sign them up, right? Well then, don't take it personally.

The neat thing about this scenario is, once your guests arrive at the meeting (just like with video pass-out), your part of the scenario is complete. The speaker does the rest (the presentation, the training, etc.). However, during the presentation, pay close attention to the speaker and watch what he/she does, because you'll be the speaker one day yourself, right?

Once again, when you're inviting someone to the opportunity presentation, don't try to explain everything to them upfront. Remember, the respect for you will not be there yet. It will, however, be there for the speaker. So, let him/her explain it to them. All you have to do is get excited and tell your prospects this is the greatest opportunity in the world.

Your excitement, combined with their *trust* in you, will be enough to get them in, and the speaker will do the rest! It's the little things you do that will make the real difference for you in the end. Do this right, because *Trust + Respect* really does equal *$uccess*.

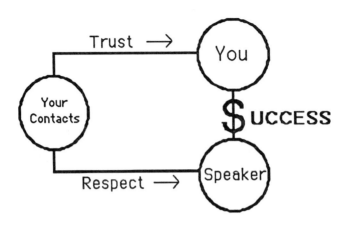

If you don't have time

to do it right,

when will you have time

to do it over?

30

Geometric Progression

Geometric progression is one of the most valuable assets of Network Marketing. It's also very powerful in the corporate world. Most people, however, don't realize its power in the corporate structure because usually only the president of the company and his/her top people reap the benefits of it.

In Network Marketing, however, whoever partakes in building a group reaps the benefits of geometric progression. The definition of geometric progression is - a series of numbers or terms, each of which is a constant multiple of the one preceding it.

Geometric progression is simply nothing more than you finding a few people to join you in business. They, in turn, find people to help them. Meanwhile, you continue to find more people for yourself. It's a simple process that keeps repeating itself. It seems small at first, but boy does it grow, and fast too! For now, however, let's take it slow.

Question: If you work real hard this upcoming month, do you think you can sign up 1 new person in your business? Of course you can. Now, next month, do you think you and your newly signed distributor could do the same thing? I would certainly hope so. This would mean that after two months' time you would have 4 people (including yourself) in your group. After the third month of repeating the same process, you would now have 8 distributors. Again, all it will take for this to happen would be for you and all your new distributors to get 1 new person each per month into the business.

Did you know that if you continued to do this for one full year, you would end up with 4,096 distributors? That's 4,096 people in your business! How many of these people would you have personally signed up yourself? 12. And look what you'd end up with. Wow!

This chart illustrates my point.

MONTH	# of PEOPLE	MONTH	# of PEOPLE
Jan.	2	July	128
Feb.	4	Aug.	256
March	8	Sept	512
April	16	Oct.	1024
May	32	Nov.	2048
June	64	Dec.	4096

Once again, these are the results you will achieve when you and everyone in your group each bring 1 new person per month into the business. Now, for most people, this will never happen. However, it's not impossible. What if you achieved only 10% of this scenario? You would still end up with over 400 people in your group! Not too shabby, huh?

When you're building your business, as you now know, you're looking for a few key people. You want to put your key people on your front line. (This simply means putting people directly underneath you.) Let's say you have 5 key distributors on your front line. Do you think they will also want to build a group for themselves? Sure they will! If you don't believe me, just ask them.

215

Now, when they find 5 key people to put on their front lines, that will give you 25 people on your second line. Further, when your second generation of distributors start building a group for themselves, here's what can happen:

You	1	You
1st Generation	5	Your 5 key front line people
2nd Generation	25	Their 5 key front line people
3rd Generation	125	And so on
4th Generation	625	And so on
5th Generation	3125	And so on

That's almost 4,000 people! You will have over 3,000 distributors on your fifth level alone! The neat thing about this is you'll probably know only a few of them personally, but that's where the majority of your income will be generated. Isn't geometric progression incredible? I knew you'd like it.

Here's another example. This one is toned down a little bit just to further demonstrate its power:

Say you started off with 5 front-line distributors in your group, just like the last scenario. These people, however, weren't as good as you. They had only 4 people each on their front line. This would give you 20 distributors on your second line instead of the 25 in the above scenario. Their distributors had only 3 people each on their front line, who in turn had only 2 people each! In this case, here's what would happen.

You	1	You
1st Generation	5	Your 5 key front line people
2nd Generation	20	Their 4 key front line people
3rd Generation	60	Their 3 key front line people
4th Generation	120	Their 2 key front line people
5th Generation	240	Their 2 key front line people

Even with this toned-down scenario, you would still end up with over 400 people in your group. The

216

key thing here is this: When the new year arrives, instead of starting with nothing, you'll already have 400 people in your group. Talk about security?! Next year, if it takes you and everyone in your group all year to find just 2 people each, you'd end up with over 1,200 people.

If you really think about it, finding 2 people each would be a joke. The results, however, are no joke. Finding 2 people each would triple your business from 400 to 1,200 people in just one year! We're talking extreme part-time efforts here, folks. What if you all found 3 people each next year? How about 4? 5? It's up to you.

As you can see, geometric progression is very powerful. I am personally very thankful for it. I would not have accomplished all that I did without the benefits of it (other people's efforts). All of the success stories you hear about in Network Marketing are, in most part, due to geometric progression.

These successful distributors built large groups and then earned percentages off their group's total volume. That's all there is to it! Once your people start building their own groups, you'll start to see the benefits of geometric progression immediately, and so will they. It will do wonders for your lifestyle, just as it already has for thousands of people in the past.

Well done

is much better than

well said.

3 1

Would You Rather have $100,000 Cash or a Penny Doubled each Day for One Month?

Most people would take the $100,000 without even thinking twice about it. That would be a huge mistake, and here's why: Most people would hear about the $100,000 and focus solely on that, without paying much attention to the rest of the offer. Here's what they'd miss out on because of their impatience and lack of foresight:

Day #	$	Day #	$$	Day #	$$$
1	.01	11	$ 10.24	21	$ 10,485.76
2	.02	12	$ 20.48	22	$ 20,971.52
3	.04	13	$ 40.96	23	$ 41,943.04
4	.08	14	$ 81.92	24	$ 83,886.08
5	.16	15	$ 163.84	25	$ 167,772.16
6	.32	16	$ 327.68	26	$ 335,544.32
7	.64	17	$ 655.36	27	$ 671,088.64
8	$ 1.28	18	$ 1,310.72	28	$ 1,342,177.28
9	$ 2.56	19	$ 2,621.44	29	$ 2,684,354.56
10	$ 5.12	20	$ 5,242.88	30	$ 5,368,709.12

What would your answer to the question be now, after seeing this chart? The penny doubled scenario, right? It doesn't look like much at first, but look at the long-term effect!

If the penny doubled scenario was your business, the first 7 days would have only earned you .64 cents. With these results, most people would say, "I should have taken the $100,000 instead." However, the people with foresight would realize, when you get something for nothing, you just haven't been billed for it yet, and would continue to build their business.

After 2 weeks, or the 14th day, you would have earned $81.92. At this point, the pessimists would quit. The optimists, on the other hand, would say, "It's not much money *yet*, but my business has increased by over 12,000% in just 1 week." That would encourage them enough to continue on. By the end of the 3rd week or the 21st day, you would have earned $10,485.76. Are you starting to see the picture now? It would take you 25 days to actually surpass the original $100,000, but by month's end, you'd be worth over $5,000,000.

This is a great example of how Network Marketing and geometric progression work. Just pretend the $100,000 is a corporate position and the penny doubled for a month is your Network Marketing business.

For most people, the corporate position would look better up front. That's because it offers a guaranteed paycheck and a decent benefit package. But does it guarantee a future? No way! Folks, it's easy to see which one offers the most security in the end - Your Network Marketing business. Of course, you have to work hard, but at least your hard work will pay off. Now, that's what I call security. How about you?

The reason why
some people don't
recognize opportunity
is because it usually
comes disguised as
hard work.

Patrick & Nicolett

Order in bulk and save.

To order more books, call us now at:

(800) 300-1177

As you can see, the more you order, the more of a discount you'll receive. Call now for fast delivery.

Books	Price Per (USA)
1	$14.95
5-9	12.95
10-24	11.95
25-99	10.95
100 or more	8.95
500 or more	6.95
1000 or more	4.95

Shipping & Handling: add $3.00 per book.
NOTE: For orders of 2 or more books, or for orders outside the USA, please call us or fax us for S & H.
TOLL FREE (800) 300-1177
Local: (610) 690-5500   Fax: (610- 690-2100

---

*Bulk discounts are also available on other training materials.

EPILOGUE

What is Unlimited Horizons Training?

Unlimited Horizons Training is a training company which specializes in Network Marketing. The company was formed in 1993 by Patrick Higgins. Patrick is a highly successful, highly motivated individual who became quite accomplished in a very short period of time in this industry.

Since 1990, Patrick has traveled all over the country and has trained hundreds of thousands of individuals from all over the world in this exciting and highly profitable industry. After countless seminars and many requests, Patrick realized it was time to share his unique and adaptable training techniques to any individual, regardless of their race, age, religion, gender, or background.

He now trains the Network Marketing industry solely, and is not locked into any one company. He is currently training reps and distributors from over 30 Network Marketing companies. Patrick specializes in training, promoting, and teaching the *truth* about Network Marketing and where it's headed to anyone who needs it. So take his approach very seriously. It will change your life.

We here at Unlimited Horizons Training have one goal - TO HELP YOU BECOME SUCCESSFUL! No one is doomed to failure at birth. All of us were all born to win! Unfortunately, we've been conditioned to lose. This fact is sad, but it doesn't have to be permanent. We just have to recondition our lives. That's why we are committed to guide and assist you in bringing out your true winning abilities. If we're successful in doing this, you'll be successful in Network Marketing. That's our main purpose.

We would very much like to do a training seminar for you and your group sometime in the near future. These training's are changing lives! After a training, the one thing we hear most is, "I get it now! I finally understand!" Patrick's training is being dubbed, "The college education of Network Marketing". You have to see it to believe it!

We are very confident this training will both *help* and *impress* you. We have already successfully trained thousands of people in the past. Now, we want to help train you and your group in the future. If you like what you've read in this book, we urge you to call. WE GUARANTEE you will not regret it.

For more information on how to set up a training, call us now at (610) 690-5500. When you call, leave a message and we will definitely get back to you. We look forward to hearing from you. Call now!